Anthony Troon established *The Scotsman Di*[illegible] in case he was being followed. He edited the column for nine years during which its shape, and his too, changed several times. Now a freelance writer, he collaborates with Bob Dewar in their satirical strip cartoon. The ex-diarist lives with Jackie in a Tayside farmhouse from where he can see anyone approaching from miles away. Born in Rosyth, Fife, in 1935, he worked as a journalist on daily newspapers and radio in Scotland and in southern Africa. He will never forget his Diary days as long as he lives.

THE BEST OF THE SCOTSMAN DIARY

THE BEST OF

THE SCOTSMAN DIARY

TONY TROON

EDINBURGH AND LONDON

in conjunction with

First published in Great Britain in 1992 by
MAINSTREAM PUBLISHING COMPANY (EDINBURGH) LTD
7 Albany Street
Edinburgh EH1 3UG

ISBN 1 85158 5079

A catalogue record for this book is available from the British Library

Typeset in Plantin by Saxon Graphics Ltd, Derby

Printed in Great Britain by Butler & Tanner Ltd, Frome

CONTENTS

There are those who think that the word *diary* is derived from the same root as *diarrhoea*, and to them I extend my heartfelt apathy after nine years of editing *The Scotsman Diary*. If a diarist doesn't vex one or two people just a wee bit, then he's not doing the job properly.

But it's the others, the *diarrhoea-ophiles*, who make the job not only possible but the most fun in journalism. They are countless readers, cynics and professional stirrers who find in the Diary a welcome relief from political pomposity and a relaxing descent into the dubious.

They are the voices on the phone, the oft-anonymous scrawls, the taps on the back in pubs. This collection of *diarrhoea* would not have been possible without them, and so to them it is dedicated. Whoever they are.

Anthony Troon, 1992

SCOTTISHNESS

THE implications of the following tale for Scottish culture and the Scottish psyche are simply enormous.

The scene is Milne's Bar, the 'poets' pub' in Hanover Street, Edinburgh, which has sheltered such great figures as Hugh MacDiarmid, Norman MacCaig and, er, Hugh MacDiarmid. The time is Friday night, before the Scotland v France rugby international.

Enter a group of French supporters decked out in the kilt. So far, so flattering: they are greeted with good-natured badinage.

One of them, however, produces a set of bagpipes, the genuine *piob mhor* of this land, and swings the drones professionally upon his shoulder. From this apparition then issues music of great subtlety and style, stunning the listeners into silence.

Well, it didn't take long for the Milne's Bar cronies to twig that he had a tape-recorder concealed about his person.

If that had been all, this would simply be another example of cross-dressing in licensed premises. But it was then discovered that this wily EC partner had adapted his pipes by removing the 'non-return valve' and filling the bag with red wine, which he was squeezing into his mouth by elbow-power.

FROM the London *Observer*. 'It is estimated that the water supplies of more than 7.5 million people in Scotland have absorbed excessive concentrations of lead.'

This must explain why there are only 5 million of us left.

THE Conservatives' famous expertise in conference organisation swung into well-oiled motion in Perth. Harvey Thomas, the 'presentations man' from the London Central Office, duly flew north with his squad of assistants to Perth City Hall, with the task of assembling the props so that the Scottish Tory Conference would be held against its usual confident and imposing backdrop.

This particular construction involved two stylised maps of Scotland, judiciously arranged to catch the TV camera lens. After these had been erected, a simple Tory rustic from the Northern fastnesses entered the hall and declared: 'Here — you've got the maps upside down.'

Moment of embarrassed silence. Then the squad moved into its famed, highly-rehearsed routine to turn the maps the right way up, while a functionary could be heard urging them, 'Quick — before the press photographers arrive!'

FETLAR, the underpopulated Shetland island that advertised for 'settlers' later set a tongue-in-cheek quiz entitled: 'Are you a fully-integrated incomer?' These were the sort of things being asked:

- How long had you lived in Shetland before you stopped referring to the place as 'the Shetlands'?
- The first time you heard Shetlanders speaking dialect, did you think they were speaking 'the Gaelic'?
- What do you miss most by living in Shetland? Daily papers every morning? Everything English (or Scottish, Welsh etc)?
- When asked to join a committee, do you agree readily — knowing that you were destined to change all of Shetland for the better?

Those scoring top marks were told they had integrated well — 'either that or you're cheating'. But lowest scorers were advised: 'Pathetic! There's only one question worth asking: why are you living here?'

THE phone rang (well, it often does) in the Scottish Information Office at New St Andrew's House, Edinburgh, where the workings of the Government are explained to the lieges. The voice on the phone said: 'Can you give me the recipe for a Forfar bridie, please?'

Consternation and double-takes. The press officer explained that the lady was speaking to a Government department. What made her think they could clue her up on bridies?

She explained that she was phoning from the south of England. She'd asked directory inquiries where might be the best source of Forfar bridie insights — and the operator found this curious entry 'Scottish Information Office'. Obviously, this meant that if you wanted to know anything about bagpipes, haggis and thick woolly socks, this was the place.

The puzzled southronette was put in touch with the Scottish Tourist Board, experts on bridies of all geographical types.

WE are indebted to the very English *Sunday Times* for solving a mystery which has puzzled Scots for generations: Who was this Jock Tamson whose bairns we are all privileged to be? Answer — he was just another blasted trendy playwright:

> **The South Bank Show**
> 10.35–11.35 p.m. ITV
> Hilary Chadwick's film follows the development of a Scottish theatre piece entitled Bairns from first readings to dress rehearsal. Written by Jock Tamson, the play takes apart the cliché of the drunken Scotsman.

ONLY the best Burns suppers avoid boring pomposity. After some unedifying roll-throwing, haggis-spillage and rude interjections at the Scotch Malt Whisky Society event in Leith, Conservative intellectual Michael Fry was assisted to an early departure, his toast to the lassies undelivered. Liz Lochhead replied nevertheless. There will be no return bout.

Another high spot was the presentation of a life membership scroll to David Daiches by Hamish Henderson the previous year's recipient. Prof Daiches responded in Bardic verse, and here are three elegant stanzas:

I never thocht that I wad be
Amang the artistocracy.
Or listed in the company
O' rich an' famous;
But noo at last I bear the gree
Alang wi' Hamish.

O Hamish, wale of Scotland's drinkers,
Your sangs are sung by toffs an' tinkers,
By usquebaugh an' tankard sinkers
At Sandy Bell's;
But ilka Scot who wears nae blinkers
Fa's for your spells.

While Scots detest their Tory rule,
While Nicky Fairbairn plays the fool,
While Lizzie Lochhead plays it cool
— A lass o'pairts —
Still Hamish Henderson will rule
O'er Scottish hairts.

THIS Scots publisher had had a tough day in Amsterdam, trying to convince various booksellers that Scottish history was very different from English history. He was dragging his weary bones along a side street when he was cornered by a tramp — and he had already found that scroungers who could beg in several languages were quite common in Amsterdam.

He had devised a way out. He looked puzzled and (drawing on his meagre Gaelic) said *Tha mi duilich* ('I am sorry').

On this occasion, however, the man's face lit up and he launched into a long one-sided conversation in Gaelic, most of which the astonished publisher couldn't understand.

He told the Diary: 'I beat a quick retreat before he burst into song. Now I'm working on "I am sorry" in Eskimo.'

THE lads and lassies from up-country will love this. Among the courses offered by the Open Learning Centre at Napier Polytechnic, Edinburgh, were '*Becket* (in French), *Le Blé en Herb* (in French), and *Ceol na Gaidhlig* (Gaelic music and poetry)' — all of them bracketed together under 'Foreign Literature'. Oh dear.

CHARLES KENNEDY MP has had his voice mistaken for that of broadcaster James Naughtie. These things happen *ad nauseam* to Scots who operate in the deep south.

But there's been a new development. Kennedy told a Glasgow conference of his appearance on a BBC Radio 1 programme, when a listening Cockney phoned in and accused him of being Robbie Coltrane. 'Git awai,' said the listener, when Kennedy protested, 'this is a wind-oop.' We hear the MP was lost for words, for a few seconds anyway.

LISTENERS to *The News Quiz* on BBC Radio 4 enjoy being regaled with curious stories from the week's press. Here is a transcript from the programme when Alan Coren, a former *Punch* editor, dredged up a real oddity:

Barry Took: And finally we come to Alan — what have you brought for us, Alan?

Coren: I've brought a cutting from the *Scotsman*, Barry . . .

Took: Oh, how nice!

Coren: . . . mmm, which tells us — although not in its original accent — that the dead dog found hanging from a tree in Bog Wood, near Penicuik [mispronounced] at the weekend was actually a fox, Lothians and Borders Police reported yesterday. They are no longer anxious to hear from anyone who has lost a ginger whippet.

(*Laughter*)

An alert Diary mole thought there was definitely something familiar about that tale. He turned his copy of *Cuttings* the pick of the 'Country Life' feature from *Punch* published in 1980. Years ago, note.

And there it was, the self-same story, from a cutting which had been sent in by an Edinburgh reader. Not only that, but *Cuttings* had inadvertently included the story twice. We have heard of a good yarn going far, but this one is definitely trying for a longevity record.

PANIC stations in the etymological departments of the non-Scottish press. It happened after those responsible for starting fires at two animal research centres were described by a Scottish firemaster as 'contemptible bampots' — a quote which was put out to the news media by the Press Association in its usual efficient way.

But they had to follow this later with a definition. 'Bampot,' they advised the ignorant, 'is a Scottish word meaning idiot.' The word is included in the new *Chambers English Dictionary*, with the note 'Ety. uncertain.'

THE auld Scots tongue is certainly a wonderful medium for slinging insults. Sir Kenneth Alexander, who is president of the Scottish National Dictionary Association, said at the hanselling in Edinburgh of *The Scots Thesaurus*: 'Our language is rich in words of abuse. Sometimes it seems to contain more insults than anything else. This makes the dictionary and the thesaurus quite invaluable.'

Then, wearing an expression of sublime innocence, Sir Ken went on to describe 'the AGM of a major British company' which he had attended. He said:

'*It was mair heeliegoleerie than ony other I have ever attended. It was a richt carfuffle. I was dumfoonert when the rauch, carnaptious maister-man said I couldnae speak. What flumgummery! If he'd gaed me lave to speak I'd have said, "Ye brosie-headit puddock! Ye've poud a stick tae brak yer ain back!"*'

What — and who — could Sir Ken be talking about? Surely not the London AGM of British Steel, when Sir Robert Scholey cold shouldered the stalwarts of the Scottish steel lobby? All he would say afterwards was: 'You'll note that I was careful not to name names.'

AND another thing: the Chancellor of the Exchequer doesn't pronounce his name properly. This revelation comes to the Diary from Professor Emeritus Gordon Donaldson, HM Historiographer in Scotland, pointing out that Norman Lamont's surname is Scandinavian in origin and means 'the lawman'. In fact, it has frequently been spelled 'Lawmont', which places the accent firmly where it belongs, on the first syllable.

Prof Donaldson says: 'When Norman Lamont's name first began to figure in news bulletins, I assumed that the mispronunciation was the fault of the BBC — which has a genius for mispronouncing Scottish names. I knew that Norman's father, a surgeon in Lerwick, had called himself *Lam*ont and that Norman's school friends had also pronounced his name properly.

'So I wrote to Norman Lamont asking him to instruct the media on the correct pronunciation. He wrote back, admitting that others had raised this with him. But he was adamant that he wanted his name spoken with the stress on the second syllable. I've since learned that the BBC Pronunciation Unit supports him, on no better ground than that the mispronunciation is his choice!'

Prof Donaldson calls this 'a rejection of ancestral Scottish heritage'. He raises the issue in a book called *A Northern Commonwealth: Scotland and Norway*. Such mispronunciations, he says, are either ignorant or obstinate attempts to obscure history.

Clearly, even Her Majesty's Chief Officers of State are not immune from the auld Scots adage 'Ah kent his faither'.

AND what did you learn at school today then, child?

How about this thoroughly enigmatic little entry, listed in a BBC TV schools programme:

AROUND SCOTLAND
see ENGLISH

TWO months after tabling a question on the official title for a citizen of Edinburgh, a city father found himself back at Square One. The answer from the chief executive was that although **Edinburgher**, **Edingburghian** and **Dunedian** were sometimes used, none had achieved acceptability.

Letters on the subject poured in from people in many parts of Britain (even Glasgow) offering their tuppenceworth of advice. He learned that for those who attended the Royal High School when it occupied the 'Scottish Assembly' building, the correct form was **Edinburghensian**. At another school, however, where the issue appeared as an exam question, the answer was given, alarmingly, as **Edwinian** as in ('Currie' — help!).

From Yorkshire, Glamorgan, Newcastle, Carnoustie etc, he received suggestions which include **Edonians, Edinaonians**, **Edindonians**, **Edlothians**, **Edinas**, **Edinburians** and **Edinburgenzians**. Fast food-related mouthfuls included **Ediners** and **Edwins Burgers**.

Does anyone care? Perhaps it's better to have no official label than one that offers possibilities for ridicule. This was summed up by one correspondent, who said she'd written to her mother in Blackpool to say she was quite willing to be an **Edinbody** if her mother agreed to be a **Blackpudlian**.

THE closes of Edinburgh's Royal Mile are world famous. Thousands of people peer down them every year, squinting through cameras. And everybody knows that *close* is the Scots word for alley.

Well, almost everybody. A reader sends us an English-produced postcard showing a picturesque gangway, with an absolutely new interpretation. The caption reads: 'Lady Stair's, close to where Roberts Burns lived in Edinburgh.'

THE mythical 'mean Scot' is a favourite theme in travel advertising. Swedish Railways ran a campaign promoting their 'two passengers for the price of one' offer — illustrated by a kilted 'Scot' hiding on a luggage rack to avoid paying.

Then there was Air France. It touted its daily services between Paris and Edinburgh or Glasgow with this argument: 'You can now fly to Scotland and back on the same day, so your Scottish hosts will be delighted they don't have to buy you dinner.' Charming.

IT must have been an interesting experience for Scottish Tourist Board chairman Ian Grant in Dumfries. He helped to launch a new bar and grill called Sawney Beane's — named after the infamous 16th-century cannibal who lived in a cave near Ballantrae with his extended family, robbing and eating passers-by.

Apparently, 'Pickled Traveller' wasn't on the menu in the new bar: but there was 'Cannibal Steak' and, who knows, the chairman might have asked for a Bloody Mary.

Ian Wallace, one of the partners opening this enterprise at the Cairndale Hotel, didn't think the idea was necessarily in bad taste.

'Look at the publicity Sweeney Todd gets,' he protested — and, after all, Mr Beane was a local chap. Too right.

THERE may be a bit of *plus ça change* about Glasgow. A writer of our acquaintance researching the subject of immigrant communities turned up this interesting snippet from the Bristol *Evening News* of 3 June 1905:

'The Glasgow police have no information regarding the threat of several Glasgow-Italians to murder the three Glasgow Members of Parliament who support the Bill for Sunday closing in Scotland and which empowers local authorities to close ice-cream shops.

'They have, however, been instituting inquiries, but so far no arrests have been made. The police say when threats of assassination are made, they do not await instructions, but inquire at once.'

Who thought that 'ice-cream wars' was a recent idea?

NOT many meat retailers have a way with words to match that of Garry Cronie, the Scottish Co-op's area butchery manager at Kirkintilloch.

His company bought the supreme champion steer from the Royal Smithfield Show, and set about rendering it into sirloin steak and mince.

With an elegant choice of phrase, Cronie described the purchase as 'a great coup'.

THE British Dental Health Foundation, based in London, had a list of dentists holding open house for 'National Smile Week'. It included one who plied pliers in what was described as 'Kyle of Lock Alfa, Rothshire'.

ANOTHER interesting twist in the little matter of pronunciation. The London *Evening Standard* reported on the sale of the Scottish island of Gigha to some English mega-millionaire, and informed readers that 'Gigha' is pronounced 'Gear'.

Well, of course, it isn't, is it? Until you realise that in the south of England, 'Gear' is mispronounced 'Gigha'.

WHEN it was European Culture Capital, Glasgow did its best to communicate with its continental brethren. The Greater Glasgow Tourist Board commissioned the translation of publicity leaflets into various European languages — with varying degrees of success.

Our Portuguese-speaking mole was charmed to discover that one translator couldn't work out the Portuguese for the adjective 'wee' — so the architectural exhibition, 'For a Wee Country', ended up in puzzling Glasguese as '*Para um Pais Wee*'.

Another interesting gaffe was that Kelvingrove Art Galleries were said to boast the finest collection of municipally owned art in *Inglaterra*. No need to translate that . . .

SEEN parked outside Scottish Tory HQ in Edinburgh — a Lada car with a window-sticker reading, 'Keep Scotland Tidy. Throw Your Rubbish Away in England.' What can this mean?

EDINBURGH publisher Gordon Wright was producing a book by nationalist academic James Halliday entitled *Scotland: A Concise History*. It seemed a good idea to reproduce within these pages the Declaration of Arbroath, sent to the Pope in 1320 by the Scottish barons — the one which says: 'So long as there shall be but one hundred of us remain alive we will never subject ourselves to the domination of the English.'

So naturally, Wright applied to the Scottish Records Office to reproduce the document. To his horror, he was referred to Her Majesty's Stationery Office in Norwich, which claims the copyright. They said — fine — but it would cost him £40.

The publisher's terse comment: 'I think it's time for another letter to the Pope.'

WITH a multitude of haggis standing by for the *sgian dubh*, some Scottish MPs complained bitterly that they were liable to miss the fun of Burns Night. Sir Hector Monro, near whose constituency the Bard caught double pneumonia, was heard suggesting that there should be no Scottish business on Burns Night or St Andrew's Day, so that Scots MPs could celebrate with their constituents.

Despite Sir Geoffrey Howe's assurance that business should be over by 7 p.m., the Scots said they'd heard that one before. But meanwhile British Midland, whose shuttles from Heathrow ferry many MPs northwards, was serving Burnsian fare on certain flights.

This raised an awful prospect for MPs who left earlyish: they could find themselves eating haggis twice in one day . . .

HISTORY has been reshuffled by the Saga Tours leaflet extolling the beauty of the countryside around Glasgow. 'It certainly inspired Robert the Bruce,' it says here, 'whose birthplace at Alloway is now a museum . . . '

TOURISM chiefs in Rabbie Burnsville were not amused, and perhaps they can't be blamed. An advertisement for the Volkswagen Passat estate said that the car's ventilation system cuts out the nastier smells of the countryside. 'Fresh air,' it bleats, 'can be preferable to fresh Ayrshire.'

Here is a recipe for misunderstanding indeed. David Chance, director of the Ayrshire and Burns Country Tourist Board, said: 'I know they are referring to Ayrshire cows — but many people may not.' He wrote what might be termed a stinking letter to the company's sales and marketing director.

OUT of the mouths of babes, sucklings and the English colour supps emerges much wisdom. *You* magazine tells us that one of the great loves of Dennis Canavan MP is 'climbing the 3,000-foot Scottish mountain of Munro'.

IN an attempt to curry local favour, the promoters of a Kincardineshire time-share thing (headquarters: Romford Road, London) breezily advertised it as 'Drumtochty — a taste of Scotland. *Slainte*!' This funny little word, they tell us, is 'a Gaelic toast, pronounced as you would *Slahncher*'. Must be how they say it in Romford Road.

CERTAIN southern prints make much dreary play of TV dramas which go out on the networks with the actors speaking in the Scots vernacular. Needs subtitles, they say disdainfully. One case was John Byrne's *Your Cheatin' Heart* on BBC.

But the complaint was confirmed in a rather odd way when Scottish Television sold *The Steamie* and *Taggart* to French TV.

Not only was it necessary to prepare subtitles in French — but before this could be done, both scripts had to be translated from Glaswegian into English.

Who said life would be easier after 1992?

AN interesting little gremlin has found its way into a summary on the leisure and hotel industry, published by a London consultancy.

Its proud boast is that 'no consultancy knows the leisure, tourism and hotel industries better'. And it is linked with 250 offices worldwide, 'each with in-depth local knowledge'.

So what's the buzz from Scotland? 'In June 1989,' pipes the brochure confidently, 'Edinburgh is proposing a 24-hour Le Mans-type event. Preliminary tests have been conducted around the track which rings Holyrood Park, adjacent to Holyrood Palace.'

Funny, we seem to remember this as an elaborate April Fool hoax, complete with diagram, in *The Scotsman Magazine* . . .

A voice from the consultancy said, ahem, he'd have to look into that.

THE following conversation was recorded on an Edinburgh parking meter. It opened with the demand: 'Yuppies go home to Hamstead'. This was corrected by the next participant, adding the missing 'p' and observing, 'Spelling — seven out of ten'. To which a third came in with, 'You spell Achiltibuie then, you smart arrogant git!'

AN architect who had enjoyed a day's sailing near Ballachulish was tuning his bagpipes before taking part in a ceilidh at the local hostelry. While he was engaged in this necessary, if unmelodic, preparation, he was approached by an irate resident, a retired naval officer described to us as a 'white settler', who complained about the noise and then attempted to halt it by 'interrupting the air supply at source' — a tactic which resulted in him being thrown off the pier into Loch Leven.

After a polite pause to make sure that the retired naval person could swim, the piper continued to the inn where he entertained a more appreciative audience with a selection of jigs, ending with an impromptu reading of *A Life on the Ocean Wave*.

GLASGOW repartee lives. An ex-public schoolboy was overheard in a pub in the so-called 'Merchant City', explaining to a largely unreceptive audience that a former pupil of Shrewsbury was known as an Old Salopian. 'I see,' yawned a merchant citizen. 'I suppose that makes you a Salopian tube?'

SO much for the cosmopolitan reputation of Aberdeen since the oil boom. A trendy café in Union Street was apparently given the name 'Café Ici'. Yet one local wifie was heard asking her chum: 'Have you tried yon Café ICI?'

IN London for a weekend of wining, dining and theatre-going, a Glasgow couple bumped into an elderly neighbour, down to see her daughter. She seemed to be hirpling rather badly. 'It's my bunions,' she confided. 'I shouldae seen the chiropodist before I left hame.'

But there's a chiropodist or two in London, reasoned her neighbours.

'Naw, I widnae risk it,' said the auld biddy. 'I want tae pit mah feet in the hauns o' a kent face.'

WE have all heard (have we not?) of the North Sea haar, defined in *Chambers English Dictionary* as 'a raw sea mist'.

Writing in British Airways' in-flight mag *High Life*, we find the English contributor John Timpson seeming to think that it's a laughing matter, and advising visitors to the Scottish capital:

> But wrap up warmly. There is an Edinburgh phenomenon known as the 'haah', which in this context is not a sound of merriment but more a cry of anguish.

LAW'N'ORDER

EXETER AIRPORT
DEPARTURES
GRAB THE GUY IN THE TRACK SUIT - THEN WE'LL GET OFF FOR A PIZZA. OVER

SLIGHT hiccup for the drugs section of the Regional Crime Squad at Exeter, who were using the latest 'covert radio' equipment as they staked out Exeter Airport. One of the team, watching a suspect, reported to his colleagues: 'The target has left the plane. He is wearing a black track suit with green shoulder flashes.'

At this point, the watcher saw one of his mates running towards him, waving his arms and shouting: 'Stop! Stop!' The transmissions were being picked up and broadcast by the airport PA system.

THE end of the life of Brian? It seemed a little like that to the police when they were handed a print-out from a computer at Edinburgh University library, one which is used regularly by undergraduates.

Excuse the spelling mistakes, but this is how it ran:

SUCIDE NOTE
Death where is your sting?
Seesaw emotions in the inner man,
erupting in volcano's of dispair.
Past failures, present sorrows, bleak future
Encompassing me like a black hand
edging me of the concrete cliff.
Standing on the Abyss of Oblivation I take my courage in both hands.
The act is commited.

Oh dear, that seemed pretty final. Was this message, left behind on a computer disk, a digital farewell? The police discovered that it had been written by a student called Brian, and got on the trail right away. They tracked his address to a flat in Wester Hailes, broke the door down, and found . . . nothing. After four days, they traced him to his mother's house.

Brian, who was very much alive, was most apologetic. He was an amateur poet, he explained to the officers. He'd recently started to write verse on the uni computer, and the disk was left there by mistake. The police breathed deeply and said, okay.

Poor Brian. Before the police knocked his door down, his flat had been broken into by professionals of another kind. The Way of the Muse is never easy.

IT was the final round-up for a luckless pigeon which found its way into Courtroom No 2 at Ayr Sheriff Court. Sheriff Robin McEwan asked his staff to catch the pesky bird and expel it before proceedings began.

But this was one slippery pigeon, and it evaded all attempts at capture. The sheriff gave up, and reconvened in Courtroom No 3.

Later that day, the court officers returned to the wild game hunt — but there was still no catching the crafty doo, which circled contemptuously above their heads.

But, eventually, someone had a brain-wave. Wasn't there an air-pistol in the building, a production in some case or other? There was. It was fetched, and Ayr's own Tom Mix took aim, bringing the pigeon down.

Unfortunately, the poor bird was only injured, and the *coup de grâce* had to be a swift wringing of the neck.

Murder in court, you could say.

SECURITY was on everyone's mind at Glasgow Sheriff Court. All solicitors appearing at this temple of justice were issued with little yellow identification badges, with the signature of the issuing officer. But because the card was on the small side, there was only room for the highly apt appellation 'Suing Officer'.

EVEN the 'Legal Notices' section, that sad limbo of the advertising firmament, is sometimes capable of a sort of dry irony:

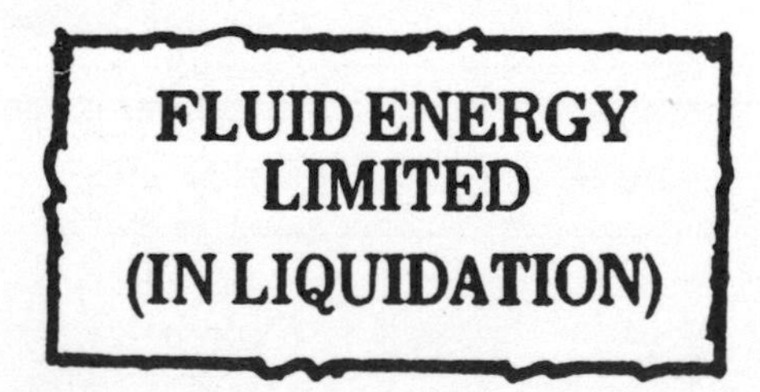

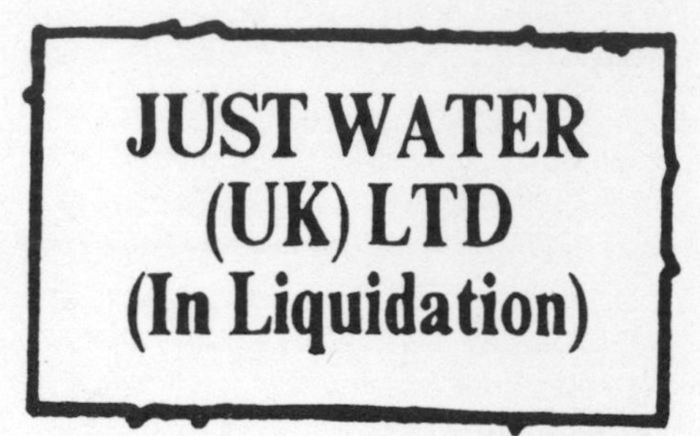

UNSCHEDULED talking point at a Burns Supper in Dallas, Moray-shire, was the fact that two participants were acquainted with one another. They were Sheriff Noel McPartlin (speaking on Burns's life as an exciseman) and Dan Ralph (who delivered *Holy Willie's Prayer*).

The day before, the latter had appeared before his distinguished fellow-speaker in his full name of Daniel John Ralph. He pled guilty to charges under the Salmon & Freshwater Fisheries (Protection) (Scotland) Act 1951, and the Inshore Fishing (Salmon and Migrating Trout) (Prohibition of Gill Net) (Scotland) Order 1986. Sheriff McPartlin fined him a total of £150. It could only happen at a Burns Supper: the Bard would have loved it.

IT would have been the booking of the decade; but two traffic policemen, operating a speed-trap on the outskirts of Jedburgh, missed a career-best by a matter of seconds.

Stepping out from behind a hedge where they had been lurking with their radar gun, the officers halted the first of a convoy of new high-performance cars being tested at a secret location in the Borders.

As the driver of the leading car was being cautioned, the rest of the convoy trickled past at little more than walking pace . . . now led by none other than Stirling Moss.

And the chance to dine out on the story that starts *'Ello, 'ello, then. Who do you think you are?* was lost. Probably for ever.

THOSE front-line troops of the poll tax, the sheriff officers, have problems of their own it seems. We heard of an elderly gentleman in Dunbar who opened his front door to admit two sheriff officers wishing to cast an eye over his furniture. He ushered them politely into his living-room, excused himself for a moment, and then reappeared with a shotgun.

The expression on his face, meanwhile, had undergone a significant change, and he chased them out of his house and down the street.

In Edinburgh's Pilton area two more officials rapped on a door. When one popped a question *vis-à-vis* the community charge, he was answered with a painfully-placed boot that caused him to double up. Another blow caused him to straighten again into an ideal position for beating a hasty retreat.

The curious thing is this: although these little cameos came to us from an impeccable source, the police said they received no complaints about them. Perhaps sheriff officers think it is all in a day's work.

SINCE law firms were allowed to advertise, they have apparently become a honeypot around which our friends of the public relations industry have been buzzing with commercial intent.

The result, according to the *Solicitors' Journal*, has been generally horrible, and lawyers were 'often paying through the nose for the paltriest of publicity'. And to illustrate the poor standard, the magazine instituted the annual 'Golden Shredder' awards.

From the zillions of handouts that poured through its letterbox, the *Solicitors' Journal* chose the most abysmal examples.

- Bristol lawyers Trump & Partners wished to advertise the fact that they had a newly qualified French (female) lawyer working for them on two months' secondment.

  The citation reads: 'Unfortunately, they consulted Andrew Buchanan Public Relations, who had her photographed next to a bell aboard the SS *Great Britain* over the line: 'Parisian "Belle" Visits Bristol Lawyers'.

  This effort won the Worst Picture Caption class.
- A runner-up for Worst Handout came from Publicity Plus of Norwich, on behalf of the Nationwide Independent Solicitors Group.

  The four-page blurb included this rather gnomic reference to the fact that the membership fees were going up: 'The group has also adopted an increased subscription scale to give action and value beyond the previous comfortable but reactive style of participation.'
- But the winner was a handout for the Scottish firm Harper's, by Staniforth PR, and was described as

'possibly one of the great all-time PR turkeys, a cornucopia of slack spelling, paltry punctuation and murky metaphor'. Part of it runs:

'Harpers solicitor Robert Hynd doffs his legal robes to don his chefs [*sic*] hat for a Scottish specialty [*sic*]: A pastry shell of section 130 Companies Act, spiced with confusion enveloping a pâté of archronism [*sic*] garnished with a soupçon of the ludicrous . . . "The recipe does provide a delicious uncertaintly [*sic*] in an area of the law where precision is of the essence," said Robert Hynd.'

And so on.

The *Solicitors' Journal* said that when the competition was announced, it 'absolutely rained dismal PR', some of the entries being forwarded by appalled solicitors and incredulous legal journalists.

A POLICEMAN'S lot is a complicated one, according to 'Dogberry' in *Police* magazine. The tale is told of two elderly ladies who went to the police station to report the loss of their car. They were so upset it took an hour to extract the details.

As usual, it took the insurance company three months to accept the car had been stolen, and to pay up. So, armed with their cheque, the ladies went to their nearest garage and were about to buy themselves a replacement when the manager entered. 'I remember you,' he said. 'When are you going to collect that little car you left for a service?'

TV cameras were allowed into Peterhead Prison to film a BBC Scotland documentary. The producer, Forbes McFall, asked an inmate, before his interview was put on film, if he'd had any experience of appearing before the cameras. 'Oh yes,' said the chap diffidently. 'In a couple of banks.'

IF you're fitting a new carpet in a bank, you usually have to do it at some unearthly hour in the morning. And that's what happened at a bank branch in Hamilton.

The fitters were trimming and hammering at 7.30 a.m. but they were also waiting for joiners to arrive to plane an inch from the bottom of an interior door.

There came a loud knocking at the outside door. After a while, one of the carpet-fitters went to open it to find four rather large men waiting impatiently.

'Plainers,' said one. 'What's going on here?'

'That's the door over there,' said the fitter. 'It needs a wee bit off the bottom.'

It took some time to get this conversation sorted out. Apparently, 'plainers' is an enforcement trade term for 'plain clothes police' and has nothing to do with joinery. The carpet-fitters had evidently set off a security alarm, and were being investigated. A case of the police starting off on the wrong tack.

THE job of Lothian Regional Council's community service order team is to ensure that offenders sentenced by the courts to carry out community service actually get down to the hard graft.

The team needed new premises in Edinburgh. It was eventually fixed up with space at the former Leith Walk bus depot, but had to share it with the social work department's vehicle park. And in that park, something like 200 cars and vans were liable to be parked every day.

This is where the problem started. The community offenders had to turn up there to clock in, to be given their allotted tasks and be issued with tools so that they could *thole their assize* to society. But unfortunately, about 90 per cent of these offenders had been sentenced for stealing cars . . . It was like holding an Alcoholics Anonymous meeting at a distillery.

As a result, the region had to erect an eight-foot high fence around the vehicles. No car actually went missing, but the vehicles were counted every night with a certain degree of care.

DRY laughter in court: an accused man, charged with stealing a car, unaccountably failed to turn up for the hearing before the sheriff in Glasgow. His solicitor was mystified. 'I'm sorry your lordship,' he apologised, 'I don't know why he's not here.'

World-weary procurator-fiscal: 'Possibly, m'lord, he couldn't find a car.'

OUR discovery of an Irish law firm with the apt name 'Argue & Phibbs' led a reader to go one better. From the Leamington Spa directory, he produced one called 'Wright Hassall & Co'.

THERE was much to be amazed about in an Edinburgh trial when Sheriff Andrew Bell was called as a witness in the court over which he normally presides. The accused was a gent who had appeared in front of him months earlier and had been sentenced to three years' imprisonment for housebreaking.

The thing was that this particular accused spat, swore, shouted and struggled in court and wore a T-shirt on which he had scrawled the message 'Rent boys f*** the judges'. And — no — he wasn't charged with libel but assault and breach of the peace.

However, there was an interesting unreported episode outside the court during this second trial. Sheriff Bell, who was waiting to give his evidence, was spotted by a duty policeman wandering in the corridor.

This is something which sheriff court cops will not tolerate: witnesses must remain until they are called in the witness room — a notorious depository of the great unwashed as they wait to give their sworn accounts of various unsavoury doings.

Was this an experience which might somehow benefit the sheriff? We hear that the policeman considered it for a split second — 'but then I thought better of it'. How wise he probably was.

WHEN Edinburgh depute fiscal Rohann Marshall 'moved for forfeiture' of a baseball bat, it was so unlikely an acquisition that Sheriff John Dean asked afterwards what exactly happened to forfeited items. The answer was that they were passed to the sheriff clerk to be either sold or destroyed.

'So,' commented the sheriff, 'we can expect a second-hand baseball bat to come on the market soon.' As an afterthought he added: 'I take it cannabis does not fall into the resale category . . . ?'

READING the minutes of a case in which a co-accused had been admonished and dismissed, Sheriff Dean noticed an odd error. The accused was said to have been *admonished and diminished*. 'If only we could,' reflected the sheriff, with the air of a man who had glimpsed an ideal world.

AREN'T our policemen . . . imaginative? Here's an interesting example:

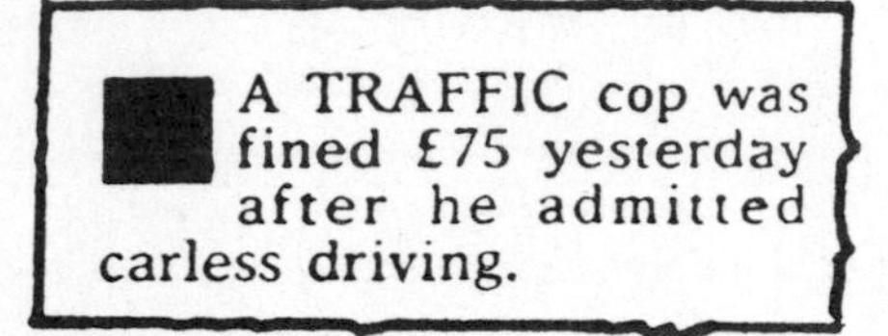
A TRAFFIC cop was fined £75 yesterday after he admitted carless driving.

COURT-ROOM drama doesn't often come in this form. The scene was the High Court in Edinburgh and the jury had been out in a perjury trial. One of the two accused had been found not guilty, a unanimous verdict. Then came the announcement of the second verdict. The script, which might have come from *Carry On Trying*, ran like this:

Clerk: And what is your verdict in the case of the second accused?

Foreman: Not guilty — unanimously.

(Much joy, tears of relief and kissy-kissy among family and friends of second accused. But the jury, muttering among themselves, pull at the foreman's sleeve and confer with him.)

Foreman: Er, I'm sorry, I seem to have got that wrong. (*Family and friends suddenly freeze*) I should have said not proven, unanimously. (*Fresh outbreak of delight and kissy-kissy.*)

Clerk, after writing the finding on his documents: Is the true verdict that you find the case against the second accused to be not proven, unanimously?

Foreman: No that's not right. (*Family and friends freeze again*) What I should have said was not proven, by a majority.

(*Family and friends gather up their things and prepare to leave the courtroom sharpish as the verdict is clearly swinging towards guilty.*)

Exeunt all, confused.

A PACKED meeting of the Ross licensing board in Dingwall was brought to a standstill by the roar of low-flying jet fighters. While fighter planes blasted noisily over the town in pairs at regular intervals, lawyers and their clients pleading their cases for late licences were forced to stand there patiently, waiting for a break in the din.

During a quiet moment, solicitor Murdoch Macphail stood up to address the board. 'I hope you will treat this application without prejudice,' he said. He was seeking a late licence for the RAF Association Club in Alness.

He got it too — but restricted to midnight closing.

AVIAN imagery took wing at Wick Sheriff Court, when evidence was being heard in a drink-driving case. The accused, a falconer, apparently tried to escape the clutches of local police by going to ground in a Caithness village.

The sheriff suggested that a falconer should surely have known that in a small community, 'there are few places to hide from the hawks of the Northern Constabulary'.

The sheriff's name: Mr David Crowe.

HEADLINE from the Press Association, which may well have a sense of humour: 'Police Stoned at Acid House Party.'

OKAY then — *Quis custodiet ipsos custodes?* (aka 'who will guard the guards themselves?'). The answer, it turns out, is Cllr David Guest, of Edinburgh District, who found himself following the activities of a traffic warden spreading mayhem and little tickets in the city's Queen Street.

At one point, the warden ignored a car parked at a meter which was registering excess charge. The councillor asked the warden why. The warden said he had 'discretion' not to issue tickets. Very interesting, thought the councillor, who then took the warden's number and wrote to the police traffic warden section.

He later received the official answer. All wardens are instructed not to issue tickets for excess charge until more than ten minutes of excess have elapsed. This is to allow for 'time clock variation' so that 'less credence can be placed on a defence that the timing mechanism was faulty'.

Now that this is in writing, defence lawyers have a new line to pursue. 'My client was aware, m'lud, that he had ten minutes' official grace before removing his vehicle. He checked the time carefully by his watch. But to his surprise, he found a ticket attached to his windscreen. The defence can only assume that the meter timing mechanism was, ah, faulty and he had been given only nine minutes.' Coming soon — at a sheriff court near you!

FAME arrived, via *Police* magazine, for a Taunton constable who parked his Panda car one night to patrol the town centre. He noticed that a local car saleroom had left some vehicles on the forecourt, and some idiot had left the keys in the ignition. He collected the keys and, for safety, posted them through the company's letterbox. 'Then,' says *Police* with malicious delight, 'he returned to his Panda and felt in his pocket for the keys . . . '

THERE was this lawyer from Kilmarnock who found himself trying to track down a client in one of the west of Scotland's most deprived council housing schemes.

Unfortunately, his detective job wasn't made any easier by the fact that the house doors didn't display any numbers, and that 'disinformers' were out on the streets helping to mislead poll tax inquiries.

However, after a lot of toing and froing about the housing estate, the lawyer did finally track down his client.

In fact, he found him at a particularly sensitive moment: the client was in the process of tearing up the floorboards to use as firewood in an attempt to keep warm. Their business didn't take too long, and the lawyer departed.

The next meeting that the lawyer had with this particular client was in his office — and to the attorney's surprise, his man clonked into the room on a pair of crutches.

The explanation was quite simple. One night he had arrived home late from the local pub, totally forgetting that he had made a large hole in the floor, and . . .

GLORY, glory, hallelujah (as the song goes). This is the solicitor's notice we never expected to see:

> JOHN BROWN
> DECEASED
> Would any person having a claim against the estate of the late John Brown who died on . . .

EVERYONE admires the way Glasgow has gone about the business of building itself a new image. It's a pity that the city's official freesheet told citizens that the Christmas decorations in George Square would feature 'ultra-violent light'.

A Peterhead prison escaper was reported to have become a born-again Christian since his recapture. But on the night of his escape from the maximum-security jail, the police did not feel they were looking for a Good Samaritan.

Coincidentally, the Royal Navy fishery protection ship HMS *Alderney* set sail from Peterhead only hours after the ex-Foreign Legionnaire made his break. An urgent radio message was received by the captain:

From Grampian Police via Flag Officer Scotland & Northern Ireland to Commanding Officer, HMS Alderney. *Prisoner escaped Peterhead Prison 1945 GMT 18 Oct 1989. Advise that you conduct search of ship. He is described as dangerous. Report when search complete.*

The ship's Master-at-Arms (senior NCO) — a large gentleman described as 'the sort of man you instinctively call Sir' — was summoned and instructed to search every nook and cranny for a possible unco-operative stowaway. He set to the task, clutching a large, blunt instrument. In naval quarters, there is a conviction that the runaway was lucky to be elsewhere; and that if the Master-at-Arms had found him, the runaway might indeed have met his Maker.

AN inquisitive journo, who found himself in the entrance hall of Edinburgh's Saughton Prison, was startled to see a poster advertising a recently refurbished tourist attraction.

It said: 'Visit Inveraray Jail'.

COURTS can be good fun, provided you are neither the pursuer nor the defender. Some examples of cross-examination at its most hilarious from the US matrimonial courts:

- Q: Did you stay all night with this man in New York?

  A: I refuse to answer that question.

Q: Did you stay all night with this man in Chicago?
A: I refuse to answer that question?
Q: Did you ever stay all night with this man in Miami?
A: No.

- Q: Are you married?
A: No, I'm divorced.
Q: What did your husband do before you divorced him?
A: A lot of things I didn't know about.

THE traditional 'Ingin Johnnie' is familiar in Scotland, with his onions looped in ropes over his bicycle. However, police in Edinburgh were seen 'moving on' two Breton salespersons who had draped their onions over the Princes Street railings to await custom.

Shrugging Gallically, they carried their merchandise to a nearby Ford XR3i, the yuppie's delight, and drove off.

UNCOUTH folk say sarky things from time to time about the amazing bloodlines of the Scottish bench and bar. Tut tut. Anyway, here is a glowing report card by Lord Dunpark, handed down in an appeal judgment:

'The learned Dean of Faculty (Alan Johnston QC) fought a valiant rearguard action to no avail, but he made more out of the evidence for the defenders than I thought was possible. I was particularly impressed by his efforts to convince us . . . ' (etc.)

It just so happens that the learned Dean of Faculty is Lord Dunpark's son. But in the best traditions of Scottish justice, this didn't help one little bit and the verdict went to the other side.

AN interesting snippet filtered through from the glittering occasion at the Edinburgh police HQ, when public-spirited citizens were officially thanked and rewarded for acts of individual bravery and heroism.

The rafters rang with their praises, and quite rightly so, in speeches of gratitude from the law-keeping hierarchy.

Sadly, not all of the heroes were able to attend. Pressure of work, modesty, that sort of thing.

There was one public-spirited citizen, however, who had a cast-iron alibi for failing to appear. Not to put too fine a point on it, he was in Saughton.

THE bad news is that a jewellery craftsman exhibiting at the Edinburgh Folk Festival discovered that someone had broken into his van.

The good news is that all his jewellery was safely on his stall in the Festival Club at the time.

The even better news is that the intruder had left behind a half-brick, a T-shirt — and a letter from his solicitors arranging representation at his upcoming trial, charged with breaking and entering. The police *were* grateful.

IRONY does not come sharper than this. Convicted murderer Michael Anderson Godwin, aged 28, successfully appealed against a verdict that would have sent him to the electric chair. Serving a life sentence at the Central Correctional Institution in

Columbia, USA, he was attempting to repair a pair of earphones connected to his TV set. He bit into a wire and was electrocuted.

He was, in fact, seated at the time — on a steel toilet set into the wall, which could hardly have been improved upon as an earth for the current. A state spokesman described it as 'a strange accident'.

TRAVEL

DELIGHTED passengers on the 8.21 Motherwell to Glasgow Central non-express were given first-hand evidence that the British Rail charm school actually works.

With Rutherglen Station still some way off, the ominous screech of brakes could be heard.

Passengers in the packed train were then privileged to eavesdrop on a business conversation between the driver and the guard — the guard's public address system having been left on accidentally.

The conversation went something like this:

'We're gonny be stoaped here fur some time. Looks like a points failure.'

'Ach, here we go again. Hoo lang d'ye think?'

'No' too lang, Ah hope.'

'"Short delay" maybe?'

'Aye, that should dae it.'

There was then a pause while the guard slipped into his Kelvinside mode to address the passengers.

'Ladies and gentlemen,' he sweet-talked, 'we regret this short delay, which is due to a points failure.'

It was the first time, says our mole, that she can recall one of these familiar announcements being greeted with roars of laughter.

NO panic, but a reader who was allowed to take his young daughter into the cockpit of a BA Boeing 757 Edinburgh-London shuttle spotted a little panel among the complex bank of navigational equipment. It was marked 'Emergency Rope'. He didn't like to ask: but to be any use at all, the thing would have to be 20,000 feet long.

TWO adventurers who sailed from Kinlochbervie to Bergen, Norway, in a 27-foot yacht went home again, firmly believing they had enjoyed an insight into Norse history. Heading for Shetland on the return journey, the *Cuan Sound*'s beam navigation broke down: but the seafarers sighted another vessel and asked if they were on course for Lerwick.

'Not by a long way,' they were told, 'but keep going and you'll reach America.'

They were given a new course. But skipper Willie Cumming is now saying he knows how the Viking longboat of Vinland the Good discovered America before Columbus: he missed the exit lane for Shetland. Should be worth a dram or two in the Kinlochbervie Hotel.

INTERESTING diversion from official business at Edinburgh licensing committee. Cllrs Steve Cardownie and

Frank Russell adjourned to Cardownie's car in the quadrangle, preparing to set off somewhere.

However, the quadrangle — a much sought-after free-parking zone for city fathers and mothers — was as usual replete with vehicles. Attempting to manoeuvre his elderly estate car to the exit, the councillor managed to trap it in a hopeless position.

Members of the licensing committee were invited to re-convene in the quadrangle to bump the rear of the car round. But Russell, seizing hold of the rear bumper, succeeded in tearing half of it off. It was a saddened Cardownie who finally made his escape, his precious vehicle in two pieces.

WE always enjoy stories about late or cancelled trains which, defying all the efforts of British Rail's publicity machine, seem to take on a sort of cult status.

This one, from an Edinburgh businessman, recalls a rather traumatic example of *getting there*. Passengers awaiting the 8 a.m. service north from King's Cross one morning were slightly put out at being asked to hang around until 8.20 before boarding.

And then, due to the cancellation of other services, several additional stops were added to the schedule, significantly increasing the journey time.

The train reached Newcastle by the time it should have been in Edinburgh. But the passengers seemed remarkably docile. They had been placated by the news that a 'customer care officer' would be coming round to take details and would offer to telephone ahead to warn employers etc of late arrival.

However, it was less than reassuring when the 'customer care officer' didn't make an appearance until an hour after scheduled arrival time in Edinburgh.

Said Our Man: 'Nevertheless, when I finally reached Waverley Station, I at least felt confident that my office had been told about the travel delay. No such luck.

'It was vaguely amusing, therefore, to receive the phone call myself shortly after I'd reached the office, telling me that my train was delayed and that I would be two hours late . . . '

THE times they are indeed a-changing. Jim Wallace, Lib Dem MP for Orkney & Shetland, was supposed to get himself up to Unst, the most northerly outpost of his constituency, for the opening of a new 'telecroft'.

These are communications centres giving people in remote communities access to computers, modems, landlines, faxes and other such useful new technology gadgets.

But Wallace was pinned down by fog in Kirkwall. No flights. So, in effect, he faxed himself up — sending a message of congratulations to be read out to the gathering.

'I hope the point of good communications is well made in this special use of the fax machine,' his message read. (Tomorrow: Royal family fax themselves on world tour?)

SHIP sinking on the M62? Heck, what next. After the signal from a nautical distress beacon was picked up by satellite, an RAF Rescue helicopter was scrambled and found itself tracking the emergency somewhere in rural Yorkshire. A United Carriers lorry was carrying a consignment of beacons across country from Birkenhead, and one of them had gone off. Flap over.

IT must have been an exciting moment for Edinburgh car buyers when they discovered a local garage apparently offering around 92 per cent off the price of a range of second-hand Fords. The 'Now' and 'Save' columns had been transposed in their ad. But we reproduce it here because it's something you may never see again in your lifetime.

WAS	NOW	SAVE
£11,077	£800	**£10,277**
£10,181	£700	**£9,481**
£9,138	£675	**£8,463**
£9,068	£675	**£8,393**
£8,828	£650	**£8,178**

MUCH has changed in the seafaring life since John Masefield published his *Salt Water Ballads* in 1902. So one of his best-known poems has been updated by Ross Westergaard in the *Northern Lighthouse Journal*. Some verses run:

I must go down to the sea again,
With my instruments glowing beside me,
With a Satnav's beep and the Weatherfax tweet,
Plus an Autopilot to guide me.

I must go down to the sea again,
With a phone on every hand,
And hidden speakers ooze music sweet —
Why, it's just like being on land.

I must go down to the sea again,
With short wave 'n VHF for listening,
And a lean roast broiling in the oven's propane
And ceramic showers glistening.

I must go down to the sea again,
To its twitter and tweet and beeping,
As the ship sails along with no help from me,
To disturb my restful sleeping.

PEOPLE frequently miss their plane. Happens quite often. Less common, perhaps, is a case of the plane missing its people — but this was the story at Dalcross Airport, Inverness.

To make things more interesting, the people included Sir Robert Cowan, chairman of the Highlands & Islands Development Board, and his deputy Philip Hamilton-Grierson. And, in effect, Sir Robert had a cheque for £1.5 million in his pocket at the time.

He was heading for Wick, where he was to announce a major expansion of the Norfrost freezer manufacturing plant, the operation which won its boss, Pat Grant, more business awards than most of us have had defrosted dinners. The cash was the board's contribution to the project.

But the Glasgow—Wick plane forgot to call at Inverness. The VIPs were left waiting for an hour before it could come for them. At least they had enough money with them for some coffee and croissants.

THERE is little, you might think, that could surprise a Naples traffic policeman. But two local *carabinieri* were slightly taken aback when they halted a speeding motor-cyclist. According to his identity card, 29-year-old Achille Dati was blind.

In court, it emerged that Dati had actually attended a training course for the blind and worked as a switchboard operator in a Naples hospital. His lawyer described his disability as a 'functional eyesight deficiency', but this did not mean he could not see well enough to drive.

A dry comment from the police was that he could certainly see well enough to do about 60 mph down a busy street. But they got him on another count: because he was supposed to be blind, he didn't have a licence.

NOT much remains of Eastern Europe as a sort of traveller's bogeyland, where visitors were regarded as suspicious until proved culpable. Take the case of the Scots author and broadcaster Kay Carmichael, who had her passport stolen while visiting Czechoslovakia.

She was fully prepared for three days of bureaucratic hassle before she was allowed to leave, followed by stern quizzing from British immigration at the other end of the journey.

To her astonishment she sailed through both control points, without let or hindrance, using her Strathclyde bus pass.

WHO'S for a very quiet time? Offering its readers an organised trip to the Outer Hebrides, the *Airdrie & Coatbridge Advertiser* promised: 'You have Sunday free to explore the fishing port of Stornoway and an optional packed lunch will be available.' Just as well.

THERE'S nothing more serious, of course, than the statistics for airline accidents. But the returns often turn up some curiosities.

An Indian Airlines Boeing 737 taking off from Gauhati came to a sudden halt when it collided with two bulls on the runway.

Nobody was hurt in the accident, but the fate of the bulls is not recorded.

Rather more alarming, however, were the circumstances under which an Ariana Afghan flight came to grief at Zabol, Iran. The *Flight International* report is quite succinct: 'Circumstances — Argument between co-pilot and security guard got out of hand; guard shot and wounded co-pilot; aircraft force-landed and overturned.'

MOTORISTS will use any ploy to get out of paying parking charges, reports the *Local Government Chronicle*. Well-tried dodges are the false 'Doctor' card and the mysteriously jammed meter. But the prize for ingenuity goes to a motorist who picked up a parking ticket in Richmond upon Thames and wrote to the chief executive with a cast-iron excuse.

He was hurrying to his car, which had five minutes' parking time left, when 'I was consumed in a heavenly glow and found myself being whisked out of the solar system by strange beings. All of the universe's secrets were revealed to me and I spent many months with the aliens until they returned me so that I could help mankind achieve happiness and global harmony.

'So suddenly, I found myself once more in Old Bridge Street; and although months had passed for me, only one hour had passed on Earth and my parking time had expired.

'Another contributing factor was that I was held up in a meeting, although I don't expect you to believe *that*.'

He got away with it, too. The ticket was cancelled.

AS the Aberdeen-Edinburgh train battled its way through Fife, the guard had a chance to display what he'd learned at charm school. The train stopped at Leuchars; two passengers boarded; it then moved forward 100 yards and stopped again. Up spake the guard: 'We are now stopped at Leuchars. If you're going to get on — get on. If you're going to get off — get off. Then we can get going again.' Nobody got on or off, but several people rustled their newspapers.

HERE'S a tale of derring-do, told by Angus MacRae at Oban when he stepped down as president of the Scottish Crofters' Union. A small island-hopping plane is about to take off — but there's a knocking in one engine. The engines slow, then rev up to try again. Same noise. This happens three times. The plane then taxis back to the shed, and the engines are switched off. Silence ensues.

After some time, a passenger asks the stewardess what's happening.

Stewardess: 'The pilot doesn't like the noise the engine's making.'

Passenger: 'So you're changing the engine?'

Stewardess: 'No. We're changing the pilot.'

THE amalgamation of the local health councils serving Caithness and Sutherland brought a huge land area into one fiefdom. Sometimes members of the watchdog council faced round trips of hundreds of miles to attend meetings: and sometimes they found themselves puzzling over the road maps.

Thus the Wick-based secretary had a brave stab at pinpointing the exact coordinates for a meeting in Dornoch when sending out the agenda. But this rather fatalistic note was added: 'Hope to see you there. I don't know where I am going either.'

WHEN you find yourself halted at traffic lights with the window wound down, the almost inevitable consequence is an earful of loud rock music from the car in the next lane. You can always wind the window up again; but in the US, it's not so simple.

The *Washington Post* reports the arrival of the 'boom car' — fitted with eight or more loudspeakers. With the volume turned up, the windows rattle and the roof shakes.

A specialist who fits the cars says that when customers want to test his workmanship, they stand outside, with the doors and windows closed, and feel the vibrating of the windscreen.

True enthusiasts give up almost all the available space in their cars to these systems. In one case a 'customised truck' had six speakers filling the cargo space, with four two-foot-long 'Bazooka sub-woofers' and another six speakers dotted around. It couldn't be used unless the engine was kept running, as it would drain the truck battery very quickly.

The boom car types have competitions called 'soundoffs', at which their systems reach 140 decibels, louder than the sound of jets taking off.

Doctors are warning of the damage this can cause: but as usual, it's falling on deaf ears.

IN a most laudable attempt to make life a little more simple for its long-suffering bus passengers, Lothian Region Transport included the following explanatory note on its bus timetable: 'Most Service 41 journeys arriving at Cramond then continue as Service 18. Similarly, most Service 41 journeys leaving Cramond arrived as Service 18.'

Thank you.

FOLLOWING a spate of flying accidents in Alaska, safety officials have identified 'Moose Spin'. It starts when passengers spot an interesting item of wildlife and ask the pilot to circle closer and closer so they can take photographs. The pilot becomes engrossed and loses control.

According to *Flight International* magazine, 'The moose has the last laugh'.

MOTORING buffs might like to know that the Rolls-Royce from which Michael Forsyth surveyed the new Dunblane bypass was a splendid Phantom from the early 1930s, now a denizen of Doune Motor Museum. But even more remarkable, perhaps, was the fact that the Scottish Office minister was being chauffeured by the car's owner, the 20th Earl of Moray, aka Lord Abernethy and Strathearn, Lord Doune, Lord St Colme, or Baron Stuart of Castle Stuart.

At the hotel lunch to celebrate the bypassing of Dunblane, Michael Forsyth was able to make some useful political capital out of this. The fact that he, a commoner, had been chauffeured by an earl showed that the 'classless society' promised by John Major had already arrived. (Pinches of salt all round, of course.)

DOZENS of Eurocrats meeting in Edinburgh to discuss transport problems were landed with one of their own when chauffeur-driven cars were provided by the Scottish Office to take them from their hotel to the conference venue. When they discovered that the distance involved was around 250 yards (sorry, metres) many opted for an easy stroll.

There are shorter trips. The Lord Provost of Glasgow, Susan Baird, was seen leaving the City Chambers in the municipal Rolls, registration G-0, to open an event in George Square. The City Chambers *are* in George Square.

SELF-DRIVE car firms are getting a little choosy. A sign has appeared above the counter of one Edinburgh company, saying fresh fish, meat and poultry are not to be transported in their cars. We can only imagine what led to this stricture.

THE art of writing smart remarks with the finger on glaur-covered vans and lorries has a long history in transport circles. A Diary reader reports this example from the back of a mud-spattered vehicle: 'Also available in white.'

THIS is at Ardnamurchan: is it the least necessary road sign in Scotland?

ONE Diary reader found himself with the following dilemma:

HERE'S an odd way of saying 'You are here'. But on the other hand, it could be a shinty score.

IT'S in places like County Tipperary that the ability to make people smile with road signs is still a living science. For example:

CURIOUS signpost in the village of North Bradley, Wiltshire. No — it's not a rugby score:

THE Orkney parish of Westray with Papa Westray is advertising in *Life & Work* for a minister. He, or indeed she, should be 'a good preacher, a good pastor and a good sailor', says the kirk session, bearing in mind the choppy half-mile of water dividing the two island communities.

This crossing is famous as the world's shortest scheduled airline route, with Loganair planes able to cut flying time to nearly a minute when the wind is in the right direction

Could be handy, perhaps?

A B R O A D

THE appearance of rat on a restaurant menu in Canton, China, was greeted with all-round shudders. But the German magazine *Der Spiegel* sent a foodie to report back on the development.

He found that the various dishes featuring this treat included fresh asparagus with rat schnitzel, casserole of rat with spring onions and ginger, steamed rat with lotus blossoms, and (to further dissuade American tourists, we suspect) braised rat à la Vietnam. The magazine's tester concluded: 'Only the strongest-stomached admirer of Chinese cuisine would ask for another helping.'

But the restaurateur, Zhang Guojon, hung in there in defence of his menu. Only clean animals from the Chinese forests were used, he said, and they bore no comparison with sewer rats from the cities. The flesh was delicate and aromatic, with a taste somewhere between duck and chicken.

That was not to say he had no problems. Despite all the chef's best efforts, 'the head stays soft and sticky, like chewing gum, and it is impossible to get it nice and crisp'.

But not to worry: the rat-meat is low in cholesterol and high in protein. So yuck in. Er, sorry, tuck in.

NOT everyone finds that the Mafia is bad for business. In Reggio Calabria, at the toe of Italy's boot, punters are actually able to make bets on how many murders the two rival 'families' will carry out in a week.

Police believe that these so-called 'Death Pools' (*Totomorti*) originated among local petrol-station managers. But the operation is now so popular that it has its own printed coupons and a supply of nicknames so that punters can avoid detection. According to a local newspaper, the £450 jackpot for predicting the number of Mafia killings over a period of three weeks was recently won by 'Jack the Ripper'.

HERE'S an offer to think about carefully. It comes from the Apollo Restaurant in Kiev, Ukraine: 'It is here that people used to do business and politics. Actors and writers, courtesans and rich apparatchiks of the former party come over to Apollo. You can get acquainted with those people at the table or at the bar.' Courtesans, indeed. Our informant says the only thing he picked up was the advertising leaflet.

IN the bicentenary year of their republic, the French wanted to acquire an example of the device which made it all possible — a guillotine. It was to form the centrepiece of an exhibition at the Conciergerie, in Paris, where Marie Antoinette was held before being taken through the streets for her execution.

But not many authentic 18th-century examples remain of the guillotine (aka 'the Widow' or 'the Nation's Razor').

Finally, one was tracked down to a museum in Bruges; but the Belgians were reluctant to let the awful thing leave the country. They finally agreed only after a personal plea from the President of the French Constitutional Council, who promised that the device would be well looked after.

And who is this man who has brought the ancient guillotine in triumph to the French capital? Robert Badinter who, as justice minister, abolished the use of the guillotine in France in 1982.

As if this were not irony enough, the Belgian model must have thought that happy days were here again and it was being recalled to duty. As workmen were dismantling it, a piece of the mechanism was dislodged, causing the blade to fall. Two men had to be treated in hospital for injuries; but luckily, their heads were still attached.

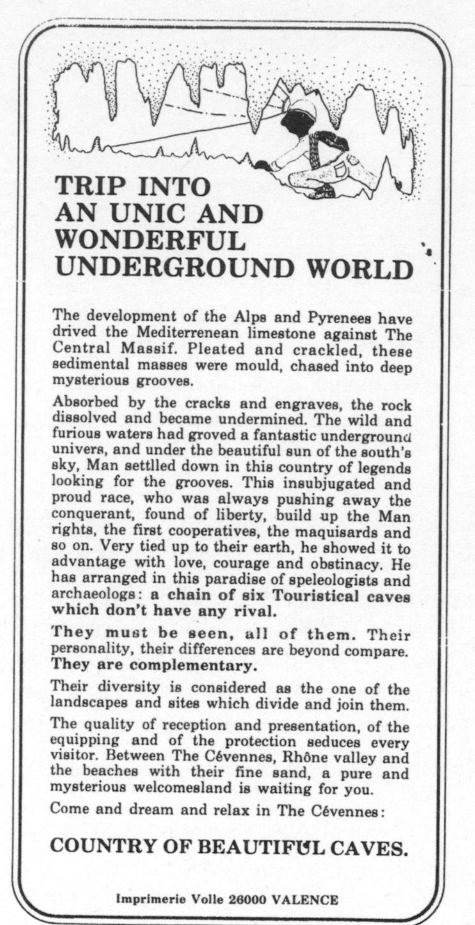

TRIP INTO
AN UNIC AND
WONDERFUL
UNDERGROUND WORLD
The development of the Alps and Pyrenees have drived the Mediterrenean limestone against The Central Massif. Pleated and crackled, these sedimental masses were mould, chased into deep mysterious grooves.
Absorbed by the cracks and engraves, the rock dissolved and became undermined. The wild and furious waters had groved a fantastic underground univers, and under the beautiful sun of the south's sky, Man settlled down in this country of legends looking for the grooves. This insubjugated and proud race, who was always pushing away the conquerant, found of liberty, build up the Man rights, the first cooperatives, the maquisards and so on. Very tied up to their earth, he showed it to advantage with love, courage and obstinacy. He has arranged in this paradise of speleologists and archaeologs: a chain of six Touristical caves which don't have any rival.
They must be seen, all of them. Their personality, their differences are beyond compare. They are complementary.
Their diversity is considered as the one of the landscapes and sites which divide and join them.
The quality of reception and presentation, of the equipping and of the protection seduces every visitor. Between The Cévennes, Rhône valley and the beaches with their fine sand, a pure and mysterious welcomesland is waiting for you.
Come and dream and relax in The Cévennes:
COUNTRY OF BEAUTIFUL CAVES.
Imprimerie Volle 26000 VALENCE

THERE was a major stushie in the 1970s over the undignified fate of James Hepburn, Earl of Bothwell, the third husband of Mary Queen of Scots, who fled to exile in Denmark in the 16th century.

For many years, his mummified body was displayed as a tourist attraction in a church near Dragsholm, the castle where he had been imprisoned on the island of Zealand. But in 1979, after complaints by Scots visitors, the dehydrated nobleman was removed from view and given a decent burial.

Now, we hear, that the 'earl' has been on the move again. A story from *Politiken Weekly* tells of a curious discovery by two police officers in northern Zealand when they flagged down a passing estate car.

They had noticed a passenger in the rear seat, wrapped in a blanket. Estate cars with commercial number-plates are not allowed to carry passengers. The driver was invited to step outside and explain himself. Who, for example, was his passenger?

'It's James Hepburn, the Earl of Bothwell,' replied the driver, who was the hotel manager from Dragsholm Castle (which has obviously been awarded a few more stars since the luckless Scot's incarceration).

There were warnings about wasting police time — until the passenger was investigated and found to be a wooden figure of the earl which formerly decorated the dungeon at Dragsholm. He was about to enjoy a career change, as the main attraction in the Bothwell Bar at the Bauneholm Hotel and Conference Centre, Hillerod.

It seemed a replacement wooden Hepburn was on duty at the castle. So after the two police officers had pocketed their notebooks, 'the earl was extended every courtesy and allowed to continue on his way'.

TAKEN from a description of the Telelavagna, a distance-learning computer system developed in Italy: 'The system is based on a few basic concepts originating from simple consideration on equipotence between source and destination, nature of the didactic message, the various phases of learning processes and the components of communication in a traditional lesson . . . '

GRENADA is widely regarded as the most friendly island in the Caribbean. Clearly, its reputation has made some impact in Ghana — for the weekly *Grenada Times* carries a rather startling column in which no fewer than six unattached Ghanaian women are appealing for pen-pals.

Their lists of 'hobbies' make rather interesting reading:

'Playing Scribble [*sic*], Monopoly, reading books and marriage . . . Swimming, music, volley, love affairs and travelling . . . Marriage affair and writing letters . . . Cricket, basketball, marriage and music . . . ' Do we detect a subtle hint somewhere?

IT seems that the Organisation of Eastern Caribbean States has discovered an interesting method of raising funds without actually increasing the tariff on imported goods. It has raised the price of its printed list of tariffs by 1,000 per cent — from $30 to $300. 'Customs brokers,' reports the *Times*, 'are crying out.'

OZOPHILES — if there are any left after what Rupert Murdoch and *Neighbours* have done for this country — will be charmed by some straight-talking journalism in the *Australian*. Reporting on a survey of illegitimacy, it belches out this stopper of a headline:

Bastard? Chances are you are a Queenslander

There's also a startling report about the tendency for people to use Darwin's main shopping street as an outside toilet. A campaigning alderman complained that on one occasion this treatment had been extended to a local bank: hence another interesting headline, '*Odd Bank Deposit Shocks Darwin*'.

It looks as if the Australian expression, *Jeez, y'wouldn't read abaht it*, is due for an overhaul.

ON the Greek island of Paxos, a reader found a shop offering 'Fresh Country-Style Bread and Grossery'. He decided, sensibly, to sample only the bread.

• At his hotel in Belamadena, Costa del Sol, another reader was reassured by a notice beside the swimming pool. It read: 'This water is tasted by the Lab of Microbiology of Sol Group Sanitary Service.'

A Poem from Strasbourg. The creator of *Ode to the Chunnel* is said to be an English MEP who suffers from insularity syndrome: rather late in the day, he (and it sounds like a he) writes:

There'll be carloads of Louises
From Parisian stripteases
Importing foul diseases
Into Kent;
There'll be modern French Wells
Fargoes
Sending juggernauts with cargoes
Of frogslegs and escargots
And men's scent.

There'll be Danes on every corner,
Faces pink after a sauna,
Trying hard to sell us porno-
Graphic books;

There'll be men like Julius Caesar
Getting in without a visa,
Careless architects from Pisa,
Bloody crooks.

There'll be Austrians with poodles
Wanting membership of Boodles,
Then demanding apple strudels
With their tea;

There'll be lecherous Kuwaitis
Driving lorryloads of Katies
From the Thames to the Euphrates
C.O.D.

There'll be men from Lithuania,
From Romania and Albania,
From Tasmania and Pennsylvania,
I've no doubt.

So dear immigration panel,
Boys in sports jackets and flannel,
Please protect our English Channel,
Throw them out!

WITH the Wall being dismantled into souvenir-sized pieces, the East Germans took to the free-market approach with gusto. Berlina Travel, the official agency for the GDR, sold the dive into democracy as a tourist attraction, offering a three-night 'East German Election Special' for £169.

'Be there as history is made!' shrieked the publicity. 'Witness the excitement at first hand! Attend the election meetings! See the campaigns! Join the world's journalists at the polling stations!' And you'll be wafted home just in time for the budget and the Mid-Staffordshire by-election . . . Haven't they heard of political apathy over there?

THE Continentals are practical if nothing else. The *Berwickshire News* reported that the tourist centre manager in Eyemouth had a letter from a Belgian couple asking (incredibly enough) for information on nudist beaches in the area; but also, they seek 'details on air and sea temperatures'.

REPORTED events at the Kennedy family compound in Palm Beach led to a ferment among readers of the *Miami Herald*. They started to compile a list of dubious collective nouns for our times, starting with 'a compound of Kennedys'.

But one reader, a PhD, submitted an entire list of suitable words:

An asylum of political refugees; a pride of egoists; a score of composers; a squabble of senior citizens; a conversion of evangelists; an incompetence of store clerks; a collection of revenue agents; an incoherence of airport announcers; a binding of underwear inspectors; an assembly of toy manufacturers (with a battery of their products); an embarrassment of Quayles.

• On that last one, American TV celeb Johnny Carson apparently said: 'There's a new poll that shows 19 per cent of American adults believe Dan Quayle is smart enough to be president. They told Dan and he said — Great! That's over half.'

IS this the reason for the West German economic miracle? A colleague taking a train to Frankfurt placed his 5 DM piece (about £1.80) into a ticket machine for a 2 DM fare. The machine spewed out his ticket, one DM, and two Irish five pence pieces — exactly the same size and weight as Deutschmark coins. Net loss to colleague: 62p.

There *was* an Irishman in the chair of the European Community, but this was a funny way to celebrate it.

PALMITOS PARK

In Maspalomas inaccessible mountains, where nobody could arrive whithout a long walk, across longs an dangers kilometres for a rustic and savage way. Today across a easy way, you can discover a natural oasis. A datepalms exotic paradise, that everybody can see. This wonder, that have been concealed during long time, can be admired now.

In a tropical ambient and surrounded of all speciments birds, the visiter can dream in the middle of nature and see many speciments almost desappeared which you could only admire in some of the most important zoologic gardens in the world. For all this the direction of the Park is very interested in protecting speciments that are in process of extinction.

Our world looses every day in natural beauty, and greens viws they are been industrial zones and caused the total extinction of animals and plants. We recomend you not to miss once you are in Gran Canaria to enjoy the nature and to spend a unforgetaole day in the middle of impressive mountains, see, this natural oasis, that will remain in your mind, like a real dream.

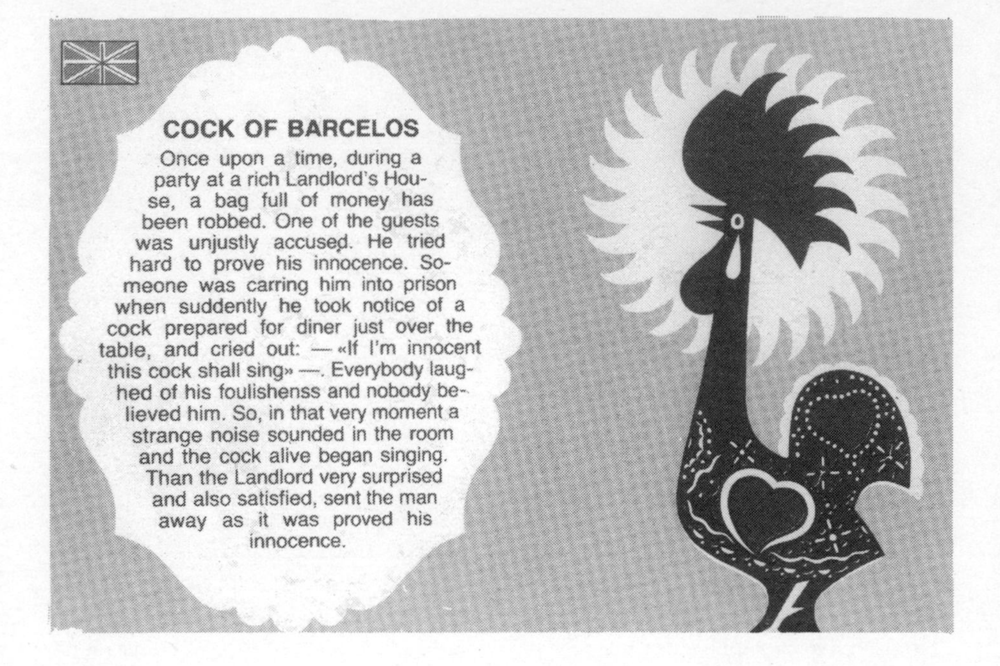
COCK OF BARCELOS

Once upon a time, during a party at a rich Landlord's House, a bag full of money has been robbed. One of the guests was unjustly accused. He tried hard to prove his innocence. Someone was carring him into prison when suddently he took notice of a cock prepared for diner just over the table, and cried out: — «If I'm innocent this cock shall sing» —. Everybody laughed of his foulishenss and nobody believed him. So, in that very moment a strange noise sounded in the room and the cock alive began singing. Than the Landlord very surprised and also satisfied, sent the man away as it was proved his innocence.

EPHEMERA from Genoa. One Scottish World Cup visitor wishing to turn his sporting mind to a seafront trampoline reports the following users' instructions: 'Before to start turning head over heels take confidence with the elasticity of the carpet; jump only with tennis shoes or without; don't put your eye glasses you jump.'

OLD habits clearly die hard among British ex-pats in Lima, Peru. Many of them spend much of their leisure time at the long-established Lima Cricket Club, where a traditional fish and chip supper is served on Saturday evenings to members and guests.

To make the occasion as realistic as possible, the fish suppers come wrapped in pages from the airmail editions of London newspapers — usually the *Times*, we hear, but sometimes the *Daily Telegraph*.

A CONFERENCE organiser setting up an international gathering in Glasgow took a phone call from an American delegate. He had a question: spouses were invited, so presumably it would be okay to bring his *possilqueue*?

The organiser was about to give advice on the lengthy quarantine period for pets, when the penny dropped. This was POSSLQ — Person of Opposite Sex Sharing Living Quarters. In that case, he said, it would be okay.

WHILE most chocolate addicts vowed to give the stuff up, the Canadian Department of Defence was actually recruiting it. With a $750,000 investment, it supported research for a new kind of chocolate bar, called the Canadian Cold-Buster.

Students at the University of Alberta helped by sitting for hours in a refrigerated room, dressed only in shorts and T-shirts. Those who had Cold-Busters to munch stood the chill for twice as long as the others. Apparently, the mixture of honey, milk protein, cocoa powder, spices, vegetable oils and carbohydrates 'helps the body mobilise its fat reserves'.

The bar was being developed as a survival aid for Arctic explorers, those who take to the lifeboats and (says Our Cynicism Correspondent) anyone stuck in a BR train in winter when the heating's gone off and the buffet is closed.

MANY and mysterious are the culinary delights that await visitors to Israel. But on a Tel Aviv restaurant menu, among the shishliks and the shakshuka, a returning reader brought news of:

Potatoes bestile with meat;
Meat Pye;
Meat cigars;
Foul beans.

Enjoy, as they say.

THE Freedom Organisation for the Right to Enjoy Passive Smoking (or whatever it calls itself) may be interested in this revolutionary new approach to fag merchandising. You might think that the cigarette name has been chosen to help those smokers who go through life claiming that they will stop one day.

But in fact, this packet was discovered by the Diary in the land of *calcio*, Italy, where the English language has such cachet that strange words are summoned willy-nilly out of the ether to give goods sales appeal.

We also saw an Italian-distilled whisky with the alluring name *Old Stone Horseman*.

And to prove that Italians enjoy a decent pun, we saw a tee-shirt craftily emblazoned *Life is a Beach*.

WHO could resist 'the family shop Petersen' at Neibull, West Germany, with its almost-unrepeatable offer: 'Take yourself time and play again! Shop around in *Spielzug-Paradies* between games, tinker supplies, dolls, automobiles, model trains and home computers. Even for a wading excursion you will find back-carriers for your baby.' The sports department stocks that essential piece of footwear for lazy sunbathers — 'a swimming boot'.

PRESUMABLY, someone is still trying to get a dialling tone from the bedroom telephone at the Hotel Relais des Champs, near Cahors, France. The instructions read:

'The Working Other is Set Out and as below — To call the circuit national and international, hang off and dial the 0 number. On dialaing sace and after the tone thoose your number.'

A HYPERMARKET in Brittany has thought fit to give its crêperie and pizzeria the far-from-salubrious name of 'Crep'n' Pizz'.

IT'S Holiday Howlers time. Diary readers returning from The Great Abroad, sent in many examples of cracked English. A high standard was achieved by the Ergife Palace Hotel, Rome, whose brochure boasts:

'The CIR-Ergife Hotel, realised by Fezia Hotels, is an architectonical unity that anticipates the future because of his conception and his struptures. All the rooms are equiped with the most modern congress equipments (!) and can be used for several purposes, as meetings, seminaries, banquets, shows with stands . . .

'You can also find a suggestive roof-garden . . . The Congressman leaves his own home only to move to another one, where he finds the best comforts of hospitality, participates in the meetings and finds a variety of amusements. Relaxing by CIR-Ergife Hotel can mean a dive in the Olympionic swimming pool. And after sporting, a sauna or a visit by the hairdresser or in discotec.'

Irresistible. Which is exactly how we found a certain holiday island:

'Tenerife is colon and sun, encient mountain with spiting fire on its heart . . . hard lands, wilderness, nearly Africans, in contrast with the colourful of the flowers; way for eassy leisure during the four seasons. Stop over on world itinerary; rock for the instant place.'

There is a hint of romantic writing in this brochure, with 'the night makes dark the sky and the earth, and even the sea, and men alights the town for the happy nightly life.'

On Crete we found a taverna offering: 'For one week only free salad or soup in your meal.' And a large souvenir shop admitting: 'Our prices are fixed.'

ONE OF Italy's more momentous statistics has been revealed in Glasgow by Sergio De Luca, oenologist with wine shippers Enotria. Giving a tasting to members of the Institute of Wines and Spirits (Scotland), he said that for the first time, Italians had consumed more milk than they did wine.

This, he pointed out, was caused by changing tastes among young people. At a family lunch, the menfolk would still do their bit by getting through three or four litres of wine. And he added: 'I don't think my grandfather has ever tasted milk in its raw state.'

• An imaginative bill of fare from an Athens restaurant:

Ornemants great plate
Bowels with origan
Utmost with irce
Smashed rotatoes
Blight
Chicken smashed pot
Bullets fry
Curled milk sheep
Homelettes smashed
Lamb spit.

WE sometimes hear about boarding-school boys, or even guests of Her Majesty, nipping off to pubs when backs are turned. Things are a little different in Russia.

Turning its back on economic gloom for a moment, the Russian news agency Tass reported the sobering experience of one Viktor Kozlov, who was attempting to enjoy a quiet drink in a beer garden in the centre of Kharkov, when someone slapped him on the back.

This is not an unusual thing to happen in a pub: but when Viktor turned round he found he had been accosted by an enormous brown bear.

According to Tass, the bear was interested in Viktor's pint. 'One can easily understand Kozlov's surprise and anger, because he had no intention to share his beer with anybody,' said the report righteously. 'However, the bear did not want to stand this inhospitable behaviour. He started a fight, bit Kozlov on the hand, drove him out of the park and captured his glass of beer and a bag of food.'

While the militia and an ambulance were being called, other drinkers tempted the bear with a three-litre jug of beer, which it accepted courteously. After downing that it fell asleep.

It turned out that the animal had escaped from a circus van, and was easily recaptured after its binge. We have to assume that later the phrase *a bear with a sore head* became more than a metaphor.

KYOTO, in Japan, looks like a mis-spelling of 'Tokyo'. Is that why this sign, seen at Kyoto railway station by a Lenzie reader, didn't turn out quite right?

WHO could resist this attraction in the Vendée in western France:

'In a natural and versant case, round a vast stretch of water made-up for your enjoyment, let's discover a fabulous aquatic equipment: the Wide Piste to come down in parties, the "Boa" unrolling its 250 meters of meanders and especially the upsetting "Kamikase" reserved for intense feeling lovers. Two heated swimming pools welcome youngs and olders.

'After these emotions you will appreciate the Snack or the calm and shaded dining areas where you will be able to have a picnic. You can expect many others surprises during this unforgettable trip.'

And how about this stern request from the management of a Rome hotel: 'Please report all leakings on the parts of the staff.'

THE most unlikely subjects are dreamed up for anthologies these days. Now we have *The Chatto Book of Dissent*, by Michael Rosen and David Widgery, whose targets are 'war and religion, racism and slavery, chauvinism and censorship' etc.

But probably the funniest entry is a people's joke from Central America, which goes:

Carlos Vides Casanova, El Salvador's Minister of Defence, is out fishing with his joint chiefs of staff; but they have no luck, not a bite all day. Finally Vides Casanova pulls up a fish, but it's very small, only about six inches long. 'That's it,' he announces, unhooking the fish, 'I'll throw this one back and we'll call it a day.'

'Please, my general, give me the fish,' says the colonel sitting next to him.

'But it's a very small fish,' the Defence Minister replies.

'Please, my general.'

'Well, all right,' says Vides Casanova, and hands over the fish.

The colonel takes its head in one hand and begins slapping it with the open palm of his other hand. 'Where are the big ones?' he shouts. 'Tell us where the big ones are . . . '

MONASTERY of Visoki Decani its the best vord of Serbian godness and the biggest and best protected monument of Serbian midle sentury art, it has build as an forgivnes st. King Stefan Dečanski (king Uroš lll. Nemanjic), and a build has been finished his son, prince Dušan Silni. The monastery had build between 1327 to 1335 year. The builder of the beautiful monastery of Dečane in Serbian-vizantian stile with the roman influence, and a gotic finesees made by fra-Vita 'Litlle brother from Kotor-King town'. The monastery has been discrabe in the living time of King Dusan. Between 1335 to 1350. Icens of Dečani include collection of them in 19 ciklus of 1000 compositions. Them were made in 'Greece Architectures' painters of Kotor in the same time they gave their cultur of painting from Roman and Seaside home of them. From the pas — to the today Dečani is the best protected and anoun monastery. Around of Dečani cames our anoun Kins and riders in the same time it become a rich monastery library and tresury. Since his mading to voday this monastery lives end works.

FROM Britanny, a container of washing-up liquid. It rejoices in the guid Scots name of Clarté.

FOR the chairman of the Campaign for Real Ale, John Cryne, taking his wife to Dublin on the day before Good Friday was not the smartest move. As he told in *What's Brewing*, they'd arrived in one of the world's great drinking cities on a religious holiday, with all the pubs shuttered.

In a hotel dining-room, however, he was surprised to be offered the wine-list. He asked the inevitable question, to be told it was okay to drink wine on a holy day so long as the honoured guests didn't mind it being served in a teapot. The Crynes ordered a pot of the house white . . . with a second pot to follow, of course.

YOU can't keep a good idea down. A Diary sybarite, holidaying on the Greek island of Poros, discovered that his local taverna was forbidden by law to serve alcohol on the Sunday of the Euro-elections, an interesting piece of legislation which has never been attempted in this country.

'But I do have some nice tea,' said the proprietor with an extravagant wink, and out came the ubiquitous pot, loaded with beer.

A cold draught of pale golden tea with a frothy head is indeed the cup that cheers, we understand.

A DIARY reader distinctly recalls going to France and discovering a soft drink called *Pschitt*. Naturally, he brought several bottles home, and his friends discussed at length why it would never catch on in this country. To this reader's amazement, his student daughter has just returned from France bringing (for the same reason) several chocolate bars labelled *Crap's*. Have the French (he asks) discovered a link between scatology and good marketing?

ANOTHER reader can confirm our long-held suspicions about scatalogical marketing. Not only did he experience *Pschitt* lemonade and *Crap's* chocolate, he also discovered *Bum* crisps.

MORE Foreign News: A tourist leaflet, optimistically labelled 'English', tells of the charms of l'Aven Armand, the subterranean caverns in southern France. 'Fantastle city of rocks,' it enthuses. 'Experimented guides invite you for a walk through the Virgin Forest, and you will discover the Palm Tree, the Turkey, the Tiger, the Cauliflower and many other figures to imagine yourselves.' Step this way, indeed.

NOTICE beside the swimming pool on a merchant ship, where most of the crew are Korean:

'Be careful of slippery all round. Please do not mischief or overaction in around pool. Cigarettes, can, bottle etc any sweepings must be get through into swepping can. Keep clean in swimming pool ourselves.'

AUSTRALIA, the land of the free? *An Carranach*, the Lochcarron community magazine, reports this forward-looking advertisement from the *Kimberley Echo* in Western Oz, seeking a caretaker:

'Drug addicts, communists, lawyers, unionists, peace freaks, conservationist weirdos, hopeless boozers, need not apply.

'We are an equal opportunity employer.'

Now read on:

INFORMACION Y CONDICIONES GENERALES

SEGUROS: Las tarifas BRAVO incluyen Seguro de Responsabilidad Civil con cantidad ilimitada, Fianza y Defensa Jurídica en España, así como daños a terceros y una cobertura contra daños al vehículo por fuego o robo. El Cliente es responsable de las primeras 70.000 pesetas por daños causados al vehículo alquilado para los grupos A, B, C, D, E; para los grupos F, G, H, I, 150.000 pesetas, y para los grupos J, K, M, N, 600.000 pesetas. BRAVO ofrece una protección adicional de 400 pesetas diarias o 2.600 pesetas semanales para los grupos A, B, C, D; 700 pesetas diarias o 4.500 semanales para los grupos E, F, G, H, I, y para el grupo M, N, 1.300 pesetas diarias u 8.800 pesetas semanales. Un seguro de daños corporales por un importe de 100/200.000 pesetas, con asistencia médico-farmacéutica ilimitada para el arrendatario, así como otras coberturas para los pasajeros, puede adquirirse mediante el pago adicional de 200 pesetas por día para todos los grupos A, B, C, D, E, F, G, H, I, y de 300 pesetas para los grupos J, M, N.

ENTREGA Y RECOGIDA: Sin cargo alguno dentro de los límites normales de la ciudad (14 kilómetros) y en horas de oficina, de 8 a 14 y de 16 a 20 horas. En domingos, festivos y sábados, a partir de las 16 horas, se cargará un suplemento de 750 pesetas en las entregas y recogidas de cada vehículo. Para poder dejar el vehículo en cualquier base colaboradora que figura en las tarifas de BRAVO y sin recargo alguno para los grupos A, B, C, D, E, F, G, H, I es necesario un **mínimo de 20 días de alquiler**; si el alquiler es inferior a los 20 días se cargará el kilometraje existente entre la base receptora hasta la central de Madrid, que para los grupos A, B, C, D, E será de 30 pesetas/kilómetro; para los grupos F, G, H, I será de 40 pesetas/kilómetro ,y para los grupos J, K, M, N será de 50 pesetas/kilómetro.

ACEITE Y ENGRASE: Todos los gastos serán reembolsados contra los recibos presentados al finalizar el alquiler.

GASOLINA Y MULTAS: Por cuenta del cliente; el cliente estará obligado a informar de cualquier sanción que le fuera impuesta en el transcurso o período de tiempo que dura el contrato al finalizar el alquiler.

IMPUESTOS: El importe total del alquiler está sujeto al pago del 4 por 100 de impuestos de Tráfico y Empresas.

PERMISO DE CONDUCIR: Se necesita el expedido por la autoridad española (mínimo, un año de antigüedad), y para los extranjeros, permiso internacional; edad mínima, 21 años, y para los grupos F, G, H, I, J, K, M, N, 25 años.

AVERIAS MECANICAS: Todas las averías ocasionadas por desgaste o fortuitas originadas en el vehículo serán por cuenta de AUTOS DE ALQUILER BRAVO, S. A., no así las que se produjeran por negligencia o desidia, o por someter el vehículo a mayor velocidad que la establecida por las autoridades competentes, siendo los gastos de reparación y paralización del vehículo por cuenta del cliente, el cual se verá obligado a abonar su importe a AUTOS DE ALQUILER BRAVO, S. A.

PAGO: Se cobrará anticipadamente el importe estimado del alquiler, con un mínimo de 15.000 pesetas, si el cliente acepta la cobertura total de daños al vehículo. En caso contrario deberá adelantar además la franquicia correspondiente. AUTOS DE ALQUILER BRAVO, S. A., acepta cualesquiera de las tarjetas de crédito con aval internacional, reservándose el derecho de pedir conformidad de las mismas al ser aceptadas como depósito del alquiler.

AUTOS DE ALQUILER BRAVO, S. A., se reserva el derecho de anular los precios establecidos en esta tarifa o incrementar los mismos, estando sujeto a la elevación del costo de precios.

INFORMATION AND GENERAL CONDITIONS

INSURANCE: BRAVO tariff include insurance of civil responsability with unlimited quantity surety and lawfull defence in Spain, so we give to a third and cover across automovile damage: by fire and rob. The customer is responsible of the first 70.000 ptas. by damage in the wages car. The groups A, B, C, D, E. 150.000 ptas. groups F, G, H, I. 600.000 ptas. groups J, K, M, N. BRAVO offer additional protection of 400 ptas. daily or 2.600 ptas. weekly. The groups A, B, C, D. 700 ptas. daily or 4.500 ptas. weekly the groups E, F, G, H, I. Insurance for phisical damage is 100/200.000 ptas. with medical assistance and unlimited medicine for the renter and also cover passenger. You can get it by additional 200 ptas. per day all tariff group, except group J, M, N. will by 300 ptas.

DELIVERY AND RETIREMENT: Without any loading inside of the normal limit o the city 14 kilometre... Office hour 8 to 14 hour, and 16 to 20 hour in Sunday and holidays and Saturday and to 16 hour to 20 hour increase 750 ptas. in delivery and retirement of etch car so you can leave the car in anyone of our association wthtout additional tax. In groups A, B, C, D, E, F, G, H, I it is necessary a minim 20 days of rent. If the rent is lover to 30 ptas. for kilometre for group A, B, C, D. The groups F, G, H, I, 40 ptas. and the groups J, K, M, N, 50 ptas.

OIL AND GREASE: The total cost will be integrate when did you Exhibit your hirig.

PETROL AND MULCT: The customer has to pay petrol and mulct and obligation to advise us any sanction when finihs the contract.

TAX: The total amount of wages has a tax of 4 % tax commerce traffic.

DRIVE LICENSE: Spanish authorities have to expend it and need minimun age 21 years old for groups F, G, H, I, J, K, M, N, 25 years old.

MECHANICS DAMAGE: All damage provoking bay wearing BRAVO will be pay BRAVO will be pay BRAVO doesn't pay damage provoking negligence or high velocity if you have damage bay high velocity or negligence the customer has to pay damage and has to pay in the moment.

PAY: We will collet prematurely the amount like deposit it will be 15.000 ptas. if the customer accept the total cover of the car or the customer will pay over respondent franchise BRAVO accept any credit car we can ask information when qe accept it like deposit for rent.

AUTOS ALQUILER BRAVO, S. A., will be increase or anulate this tariff pric if the cost of life will be increase.

SALTO ANGEL

In this' Expedition you will know the highets waterfall in the worlf. From Canaima, trough the Sabana, the Jungle and the rivers Carrao & Churún, you'll enjoy one of the biggets emotions in this life. All the facihties Camp. Guides an Natives, all experts will bring you trough troubles waters, just where a few have made it. Be you one of them, Meals ni open fire never taste so goo. DAYS. To arrange with the group.

Duration - 4 days, 3 mights. Includes transfers from Canaima, lodging and meals, minimun of 6 persons.
Cost per sperson Bs.. . . . . 3.000,oo
Aprobado por Corpoturismo 87-0733.

PROTECT THE PARK

MAKE CANAIMA NATIONAL PARK YOUR AND HAVE A GOODTIME.

IN China with a trade delegation, a Scottish businessman found himself talking to a language specialist whose name appeared to be Mr Whing. He was the author of a book of English colloquialisms for Chinese readers.

During the discussion, one member of the party indicated that he required to go to the gents. 'Aha,' said Mr Whing knowledgeably, 'you're going to bang your head.' Pause for confused silence . . .

The explanation was this: Mr Whing had met a previous trade mission and was on the spot when one of the visitors felt the call of nature. He returned to the group later complaining that he had banged his head. This had been due to a low beam in the toilet: but by this time Mr Whing had whipped out his notebook and jotted down 'Going to toilet = banging your head'.

The strange *non-sequitur* is now enshrined for all time in Mr Whing's guide to the perils of spoken English. Members of the Diplomatic Corps etc should bear this in mind.

HARD times indeed for Santa Claus in Kaikohe, New Zealand. The white-bearded, red-coated philanthropist was handing out balloons and sweets at the town's parade to mark the start of the Christmas season.

But his supplies ran out and the children turned nasty, swearing and kicking at their hero. Some parents became aggressive too, asking whether this was yet another government budget cut. The saddened Santa, something of a sociologist evidently, put the incident down to 'hard times, especially among welfare beneficiaries'.

WHEN the British hostages were streaming home from the Gulf, a thought from a certain Russian female member of the 'human shield'.

Interviewed by her local paper about her enforced stay in the Iraqi capital, she said that she had few complaints.

She much preferred Baghdad to Kiev.

SEX

THIS insurance claim must have made fascinating reading. An Italian couple were seeking damages from an insurance company for an unintended pregnancy, plus the costs for their shotgun wedding, after another car had crashed into their stationary vehicle.

The two were in the throes of passion when the obviously distracted driver of the second car crashed into theirs at the decisive moment, resulting in two accidents.

COMMUNITY workers in Edinburgh's Fort ward were thinking up ploys for keeping everyone fit and well. In particular, they invited participants to an *Over-Fifties Genital Exercise Group*. But before the stampede forms, the letter should have read *Gentle* exercise.

A READER found an advertisement from *Reader's Digest* telling us: 'Visiting your local pharmacy provides one-stop shopping for new babies.'

Our contributor, a man of the cloth, thought this a hygienic alternative to the 'under a gooseberry bush' system.

IT'S a *sair fecht* in the equality business. Take the case of the poor, misunderstood editor of *Newsround*, the quarterly magazine for employees of Lothian Region.

The magazine used a front cover photograph of the Lothian and Borders Fire Brigade 'Crucial Crew' team, consisting of five men and one woman. The men were standing like stookies — but the woman, Joy Innes, was shown kicking her leg in the air, a stock device of tabloid photographers everywhere.

As a result, the editor of *Newsround* took a lot of flak. There were accusations of sexism for printing this 'outrageous' photograph; and complaints were made directly to the region's women's unit. But in the following issue of the magazine, there was a spirited defence from the editor . . . Dawn Dresser. (Yes, a woman.) She pointed out that Joy kicked her leg in the air from pure exuberance, without being asked. And in fact, the photographer was a woman too.

How to explain this puzzling Contradiction of Our Times? Dawn Dresser told the Diary that most of the complaints must have come from humourless radical feminists. But when she phoned Joy (The Kicker) Innes to get her version, she got a very witty reply to the effect that Joy's husband felt the men should have been wearing short skirts and suspenders while Joy should have been in a kaftan and yashmak.

But it didn't stop there. The next issue's 'social work' cover illustration showed a black mother cuddling her child. Poor Dawn had a four-page letter from a reader suggesting this was racism and she'd be reported to the equality unit.

Next?

THE village tearoom in Muthill, near Crieff, displays a notice saying:

TOILET

For sitting-down customers only.

CHOOSING a name for a book must be the most pleasurable part of the writing process. (In fact, we have heard of 'authors' who have dreamed up great bestseller titles but have never got down to the actual writing.)

But Evelyn Glennie, the wonderful Scots percussionist who managed to overcome her profound deafness to become a famous musician, chose for her autobiography a title which summed up the story in two words: *Good Vibrations*.

We earnestly hope that this book was the one that admirers brought to her to be autographed: for a sort of competitor appeared in the list of titles for another publisher.

We quote: '*Good Vibrations*. The complete guide to sex aids and erotic toys. Suzie Hayman, agony aunt, counsellor and writer, is working with the Family Planning Association to write a helpful book on erotic toys and other ways to make sex more fun.'

POST-FEMINIST reaction took root at Edinburgh University's law faculty. This followed a display of posters advertising a new women-only discussion group — which, in the current climate, caused snorts of outrage among certain L-plate advocates.

They hit back by displaying posters promoting a discussion group for men. Topics on the agenda included: 'Women, how to keep 'em at the sink' and 'PMT, is it really as bad as they say?'. Outrage! The men's group was supposed to be a spoof, but a serious poster-shredding war was the result.

SEXISM is alive and well and living in Lochcarron. The community newspaper *An Carranach* published this short essay which tells us why ships are always referred to in the feminine gender:

'A ship is called "she" because there is always a great deal of bustle about her. There is usually a gang of men about; she has a waist and stays; it takes a lot of paint to keep her good-looking; it is not the initial expense that breaks you — it is the upkeep; she can be all decked out; it takes an experienced man to handle her correctly; and without a man at the helm she is absolutely uncontrollable; she shows her topsides and hides her bottom; and when coming into port she always heads for the buoys.'

The writer took the precaution of signing this piece with initials only, we couldn't help noting.

THEN a Diary reader recalled a trip up the Norwegian coastline in a ship whose master was a friend of his.

During one conversation, the captain interrupted him by saying:

'Please — you should not call this ship "she".'

'Why not?'

'Because,' said the master, 'he is a mailboat.'

Geddit?

SOME daughters do 'ave them. There's not much that can be added to this slightly less-than-romantic wedding notice in the *Stirling Observer*:

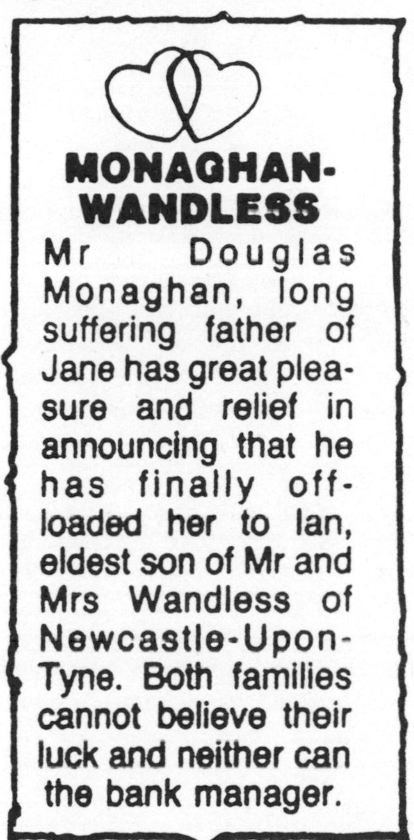

MONAGHAN-WANDLESS

Mr Douglas Monaghan, long suffering father of Jane has great pleasure and relief in announcing that he has finally off-loaded her to Ian, eldest son of Mr and Mrs Wandless of Newcastle-Upon-Tyne. Both families cannot believe their luck and neither can the bank manager.

FEMINISTS and other sensitive souls are a little obsessed, perhaps, with the titles 'Mrs' and 'Miss' which indicate the marital status of the bearer. Hence the cleverly devised and uninformative 'Ms', which enjoyed a vogue in this country.

But here's a salutary tale from the European Parliament, where similar anxieties seem to have been rife. It produced a new staff telephone directory, and because French is the standard language, it has had to avoid the tell-tale use of 'Madame' or 'Mademoiselle'. It has done this by reducing them both to the abbreviation 'Mad'.

Approximately half of the European parliamentary staff were said to be not entirely pleased.

A SURVEY showed that some health authorities were promoting vasectomies for low-income families only. So *New Woman* reported righteously: 'The NHS has told DHAs that they're not allowed to means-test patients, but where they make cuts is largely their own decision.'

Well, thank goodness for that.

PRIORITIES seemed to be changing in the Northern Isles. The *Community Enterprise News* told of events on the Orkney island of Eday, whose tourism slogan is 'Escape to the peace of a traditional crofting community'.

The local community co-op installed three condom-dispensers — two at the heritage centre and one at the pier.

Eday's fearless reporter said in the paper: 'Today, the boat carrying the fresh milk and bread and meat was cancelled, due to the gales. But don't worry — the condoms have arrived.'

The outside world boggles.

ON A fact-finding visit to Germany, a gaggle of Scottish Tories visited the birthplace of the composer George Frederick Handel, in Halle.

There they discovered a plaque in memory of another German composer, Samuel Scheidt. (You have to pronounce this interesting name to understand its full impact.) It seems that there was some ribaldry.

Then one of the party said he'd certainly heard of this musician before. 'One of my kids came home the other night and said he'd been to a Scheidt concert.'

SOME of Johannesburg's plusher hotels banned women who were sent by escort agencies to meet their 'dates' in the lobby. The women were readily identifiable. 'They stroll in casually,' said a hotel worker, 'wearing a few centimetres of clothing and with a credit card machine under one arm.'

The hotel companies believed that escort agencies were often fronts for prostitution — for which payment is now acceptable through credit cards, in the best 'that'll do nicely' tradition. However, the sight of the machines (not the women) apparently upset other guests, hence the ban. Latest news: the girls are now carrying the gadgets in oversized handbags.

WE were happy to note that for Kevin, life may be a little less complicated in future:

> Kevin, a business graduate, joined Wm Low after spending sex years with Waverley Vintners where he worked latterly as wine manager.

WAS it a sign of the times? Or were they just playing for safety? Lothian Region's education department sent a circular to head teachers of their secondary schools under the heading — 'Pregnant Pupils: Curricular Activities'.

It pointed out that officials had been discussing the region's advice to employees on the use of computer technology and the extent to which teaching staff and pupils were aware of activities and substances which can be 'harmful doing [*sic*] pregnancy'.

The department was particularly anxious that pregnant pupils should be aware of this advice, so that they were not put at risk. They drew attention to the code of practice on computer technology. 'The evidence of risk from VDU screens (computers, video and television) is inconclusive; however, where there is concern expressed by the pupil, it must be treated both seriously and sympathetically.'

In science subjects, 'where safety regulations are applied there will be no particular danger to pupils who are pregnant', observed the circular calmly. And in exercise classes, teachers should be aware of 'the possible unsuitability of more vigorous exercise, in particular where the pupil feels under pressure to participate or keep up with others'.

Sex education seems to have moved on a bit.

WHAT next? We were sent a copy of the menu from an authentic Scottish pizza-pub in Oslo. No relation, but it's called The Scotsman and its fare included the No 1 Scotsman Original, the No 2 Macay Spesial (*sic*) and the No 10 Cutty Sark, which seemed to include no whisky.

For alternative pleasures, it seems, you could go here:

Prins Charls
VISE PUB
Med interna-
sjonale
visesangere
hver aften

ONE of those perplexing oddities of the pressure group sub-culture surfaced at Lothian Region. In an expression of solidarity and all that, three key women applied to be delegates at a 'Black Women's Conference', to be held in London. But curiously, only one was accepted.

This was the region's women's officer (who is black). Those turned down were Helen Graham, 'chair' of the women's committee, and her deputy Jane Mitchell (who are white). Some coincidences are a little more puzzling than others, perhaps.

GREAT NEOLOGISMS:
Kleptocracy (n), a régime whose leaders give higher priority to the acquisition of personal wealth than to their people's welfare;
Gastroporn (n), the vast range of cookery books pandering to exotic or esoteric tastes.

(Source: Christopher Harvie, Professor of British and Irish History at the University of Tubingen, at a conference organised by Edinburgh University's Centre for Theology and Public Issues.)

THE Penguin Café, a new Edinburgh eaterie, was full of quotes: 185 of them in fact. The design consultant, Ken McCulloch, apparently hired a London historian to plough through the dictionaries of quotations and a London 'art house' to come up with suitable illustrations.

The results, framed upon the walls, included:

'A rich man's joke is always funny' (T. E. Brown)

'There is no such thing as a *little* garlic' (Arthur Baer)

'Americans can eat garbage provided you sprinkle it liberally with ketchup' (Henry Miller)

Much fun. But in a restaurant whose flamboyant motto, emblazoned along the wall, is 'Let The Good Times Roll', we also have this bitchy quote from Bette Davis: 'She's the original good time that was had by everyone.'

CAUGHT out in the country, miles away from a toilet, the usual practice is to retreat behind the nearest clump of bushes.

But it seems that in Inverness this principle was to be adopted for urban use:

> **INVERNESS district's environmental health committee will be asked at tonight's meeting to recommend the replacement of a century-old men's public toilet at the junction of Church Lane and Bank Street with a raised shrub bed.**

THE unit of currency in Hungary is the forint, usually abbreviated to 'ft'. But it was nevertheless an astonished Scots reader who saw the following sign on a slot machine in his Budapest hotel: '20 ft condoms'.

THE story so far: This young lady was appearing at Kirkcudbright Sheriff Court, where she was ultimately put on probation for two years. She had admitted stealing two china figurines from a shop in Castle Douglas. But, according to the *Galloway News*, drama was to intervene. *Now read on* . . .

> pled guilty at an earlier hearing to stealing the figurines from Scope Furnishings Ltd, 146 King Street, on September 10 this year, and also guilty to struggling with PC Stephen Stiff.
>
> The court heard that Lucas was now pregnant.

WHY are more men wearing shorts nowadays, did you ask? The Communist Party's now defunct theoretical journal, *Marxism Today*, answered that one.

Things have changed, it said, from the time when 'wearing shorts promiscuously signalled patterns of behaviour and identity incompatible with the serious business — the cultural and moral mission — of white, heterosexual, middle-class, English hegemonic masculinity.'

(Indeed they have.)

'For the pessimist,' *Marxism Today* told us, 'if the shift into shorts represents anything at all it will be seen as no more than an index of post-modern politics where signs reflect neither fixed political commitments, nor clearly readable class, race or national identities . . .

'. . . It opens the possibility of conceiving of masculinities that are not wholly organised as defensive denials of inner uncertainty, incompetence, and the ambiguous experience of gender and desire that hegemonic masculinity has always coded as childish, feminine and foreign.'

And we simply thought men wore shorts because it was hot.

THE controversy over Britain's fightin', seagoin' Wrens had a curious echo in the United States, where military persons were trying to come to terms with the combat role of women in Panama.

The *Armed Forces Journal International* resurrected a quip by former Congressman Bill Chappell, who complained about the view held in some circles that 'women can't fight'. His dry — if chauvinistic — observation was: 'Anybody who is married will question that.'

THE infamous girls of St Trinian's have had it. For the modern co-educational approach, this place in Somerset sounds about right:

THE *BMA News Review* carried out a sort of exploratory operation on medical humour. One joke came from a little while back. It concerns the advice given by the court physician to the king's favourite courtesan: 'Just stay on your feet for a couple of days more and we'll have you back in bed in no time.'

Media doctor David Devlin told the one about St Peter ringing up a psychiatrist and saying: 'Could you come and have a look at God for me? He keeps thinking that he's a St Thomas's consultant.'

THE much-respected *Nature* magazine seemed to be trying to claim a slice of the *Sunday Sport* market by giving advance notice of an article entitled 'Genetics: Depravity and Exotic Sex in Bacteria'. We learned that 'mutant Escherichia coli bacteria can have sex with another species, Salmonella typhimurium, 1,000 times more successfully than non-mutant strains'. We were not promised photographs.

NO one is more aware of 'sexual orientation' than some local authorities. They raise the subject every time they advertise for staff — saying, of course, that it doesn't matter.

The obsession invaded the Tenant Participation Advisory Service, holding a conference at Inverness. Delegates were warned in advance: 'If you cannot attend and wish to nominate a replacement, please note that your replacement must be of the same sex as yourself as we have allocated particular rooms and sharing arrangements which *cannot* accommodate any changes in the sexual orientation of delegates at this late stage.'

Does this mean that any delegate who came out of the closet (or, indeed, went into it) before the event should contact the service and confess? Might have been an interesting conference after all.

EVERYONE knows islands are interesting places. But what happened on Bressay, Shetland, to need this little reminder?

THE shaky-hands people at last found their ideal venue. The team from Edinburgh University, investigating hand-tremor and its relationship to working stress, carried out surveys in various locations (including, memorably, *The Scotsman*'s editorial department).

Then it set up its stand at the General Assembly of the Church of Scotland, where the twitches of the Fathers and Brethren were solemnly measured.

The research was done in part of the Assembly Hall set aside as a refectory for commissioners. Sometimes, this space is called the Society of Friends Hall. But as the Revd Dr Finlay Macdonald, convener of the business committee, remarked: 'Under the circumstances, perhaps, we should refer to it by its more familiar name of the Quakers Hall.'

AN EVENING newspaper at last came up with a radical alternative to those 'spot the ball' competitions. The rules weren't explained, but this is how it was described:

ARTS

EVERY art-lover's nightmare came true for the chap admiring the exhibition in The Scottish Gallery, in Edinburgh's George Street. He stepped back to get a better look at the paintings . . . and he knocked over a tasteful display of ceramic vases.

Other browsers in the gallery froze in horror, we hear, as three large and rather expensive pots by David Roberts hit the floor and smashed into pieces. Approximately £1800-worth of pieces.

It was a sad cameo which might have appealed to Bateman, the celebrated cartoonist who immortalised the embarrassing moment.

The gallery's ceramics specialist, Amanda Game, told us, 'It was a genuine accident and the poor man was very apologetic. You can't just say — "Well, that'll be £1800 please."

'We are insured against accidents, of course, and I phoned the artist right away. He was quite philosophical, and said that we all break things now and then.'

But no doubt somebody, somewhere, isn't sleeping too well these nights.

WE could only hope that the organisers of a craft fair in Dingwall relented and let a few people in. The *Ross-shire Journal* gave details thus:

FRIDAY, 20th JULY
11 a.m. to 8 p.m.
No admission

THERE was a decidedly salty air to the programme to be performed by the Royal Scottish National Orchestra in Glasgow. It started with Wagner's *The Flying Dutchman* overture, went on to Debussy's *La Mer*, and splashed down with Vaughan Williams's *A Sea Symphony*.

Not a programme for a landlubber; so naturally it was conducted by Christopher Seaman.

ALICE, that nice little girl of Lewis Carroll's, was throwing a really awful tantrum. There was a large model of the Wonderland wanderer in Glasgow's McLellan Galleries, where she welcomed visitors to *The Art Machine* exhibition.

She did this by letting her neck grow slowly, until she was nearly seven feet tall. Then the neck shrunk back again to normal, as described by Carroll in his Victorian tale of magical adventures.

The electric motor which produced this effect was situated, very decorously, under the young lady's skirt.

But some of the younger visitors to the exhibition, it seems, became rather too friendly with Alice. The official version was that they insisted on shaking her hand — although there's a strong suggestion that she was being treated with much greater familiarity.

Anyway, Alice reacted indignantly by shooting her neck out to its fullest extent and then withdrawing it into her shoulders where it hunched at an unnatural angle.

In short, she blew up.

The floor manager of the exhibition, Jilly Anne Healey, called a technician. He fiddled around under Alice's skirt in a vain attempt to repair the motor — in which compromising position, we hear, some of the staff took his photograph.

But Alice simply refused to co-operate, and was out of action for a week while her designer was called in to placate her.

When she returned to duty, the organisers put a little rope barrier around her to keep her amorous admirers at a distance.

HERE'S an insight into the public entertainment licence business. Edinburgh's licensing sub-committee met to consider various applications, including one for Van Morrison and Runrig concerts to take place on the Castle Esplanade.

The committee seemed to like the sound of these gigs. Much was said about how the Esplanade could become a venue for similar guitar-thrashing in the future. Application approved, no worries.

Afterwards, it emerged that three members of the licensing committee, an environmental health official and the committee clerk had already bought themselves tickets for these events. There seems to be some sort of moral here, but you'll have to work it out for yourselves.

THERE are no holds barred in the kiddy book review business. *Books Ireland* hired reviewers aged from seven upwards to assess the latest on the shelves for young people. They were rewarded with some marvellous put-downs, spiced with rampant ageism. For example:

Fionuala the Glendalough Goat (suitable for 8–10-year-olds): 'You would definitely think it is for a younger person, judging by the cover.' — Lucy, 9.

Cornelius in Charge: 'When you look at the cover you would think it was babyish and for about 7-year-olds until you see the thickness. Then you think it is for 9-year-olds. Really it is for 9 to 10 years.' — Madeleine, 10.

Daisy Chain War (for teenagers): 'Not very good. The language would be suited to 10-year-olds; maybe the subject-matter to 13 or 14-year-olds. Poor story line. Really bad.' — Stephen, 13.

The Poolbeg Children's Quiz Book No 3: 'The questions for the older ones were easy. I didn't have to look back for the answers.' — Andrew, 10.

But for the ultimate put-down, we have *The Sea of Possibility*, as reviewed by Daniel, 14: 'It's quite good, but you wouldn't read it unless you were very bored.'

IT was an unusual departure for top jazz singer Carol Kidd. At a glittering sponsored concert in Edinburgh (splendid supper afterwards in the Signet Library and all that) the Glasgow-born lassie decided to sing the traditional 16-bar blues *Trouble in Mind*, which includes the suicidal lyrics:

Gonna lay my head
On some lonesome railway line;
Let that 2.19 train
Pacify my mind.

Unfortunate, perhaps — considering that the sponsors happened to be British Rail's Inter-City organisation and the gallery of the Queen's Hall was packed with their top executives and guests. But, we were assured, this was no part of the official BR user-friendly message.

THE Diary ran a competition to choose apt business sponsors for popular songs and many good ideas didn't make the winning six. For example, we had the deliciously sexist *Move Over Darling* (British School of Motoring) from an Edinburgh reader, and *I've Got You Under My Skin* (Ethicon Ltd, the surgical suture manufacturers) from Kelso. Other readers sent us *I Hear You Knocking (But You Can't Come In)* sponsored by the Masonic Lodge, and *I Close My Eyes and Count to Ten* by the British Boxing Board of Control. But for better or worse, these were our winners:

Next! (British Dental Association).

It's Over (British Steel).

They Can't Take That Away from Me (Securicor).

Bye Bye Blues (The Labour Party).

Great Balls of Fire (The Vasectomy Clinic).

You're Driving Me Crazy (British School of Motoring).

And here are some more cheeky ideas:

Train is a-coming — Oh Yes (ScotRail).

It's Not Unusual (Gay Rights).

The Way We Were (Aberdeen FC).

I Can't Get Started (Automobile Association).

Where Have All the Flowers Gone? (Edinburgh Parks Dept).

You Go to My Head (Isle of Skye Whisky).

Good grief: someone even discovered that the song *Ebb Tide* was actually composed by one Robert Maxwell; while others suggested that the pillaged Mirror Group Pension Fund should sponsor *When I'm 64* and *We'll Meet Again*.

Dreadful.

GRAVE news from *Melody Maker*, required reading of electric guitar bashers etc. A campaign was afoot to end a plague of violence at gigs, with people seeking to do harm to the band, themselves and others. It was particularly noticeable, the magazine said with unconscious irony, during a tour by Slayer and Overkill.

UNFORTUNATELY, we missed the special sound effects which were promised when the Edinburgh choir Bel Canto gave a recital of Spanish Renaissance motets at the National Gallery.

The notice read: 'Mulled wine and mince pies will be served in the entrance hall, where the acoustics are particularly fine.'

THE *samizdat* style *Glasgow Keelie*, whose aim was to save the city from yuppification and return it to the workers, reached a healthy fourth issue.

Among much denigration of leading Labourites, Cllrs Pat Lally and Jean McFadden ('Doolally . . . McBadyin'), there was also this rather tasteful logo — which the Diary first saw being worn on a T-shirt in Inverness, believe it or not:

INTERESTING Freudian slip by teenage actress Lorraine Pilkington, telling *meejavolk* in London about rehearsals for her first part at Dublin's Abbey Theatre. It was in Sean O'Casey's *The Plough and the Stars*. Inspired by the farming connotation, she said the production was part of Dublin's year as 'European City of Agriculture'.

IT'S NEW. It's different. And it would have come in useful at those Festival receptions where the guests wander round with glasses of wine clipped to their plates. It's the 'Tie Protector', offered by a gifts company in the section mis-spelled 'Executive Aquisitions'.

It's clipped horizontally across the gent's necktie, below the knot. When the time comes to dig into his spaghetti, he pulls down the 'polka-dot plastic' bib which unrolls like a window blind. Somehow, the model shown wearing it manages to keep a straight face.

KEVIN COSTNER'S *Dances with Wolves* may well have won seven Oscars, but it didn't get the award for immaculate timing. That's the view of Edinburgh audiences who sat through the three-hour epic in a city cinema.

Because of the length of the film, there was one intermission. Just before the break, there's a scene where the Sioux have killed a buffalo. The animal's heart is torn out: the high heid injun takes a bite at it and hands the dripping organ to Costner who, after a moment's doubt, sinks his teeth into it.

Then, with the audience gagging, the lights go up and a screen commercial attempts to sell hot dogs . . .

TED HUGHES didn't write the poem to the Forth Bridge everyone was hoping for. What the Poet Laureate penned was a letter.

The Forth Bridge Centenary Trust asked Hughes if he would do the honours with a few couplets. But he politely declined, saying he would feel 'like a tinker' looking at the bridge.

However, the Scottish Poetry Library dug out a hitherto unpublished work by young Edinburgh poet Colin Donati — and this was received with enthusiasm by the trust's chairman, Lord Elgin.

Then Sheila Mackay, author and publisher of the official centenary book *The Forth Bridge* sent a copy of Donati's poem to Huges and received a reply. A letter from a Poet Laureate, of course, is an ode in itself . . .

Dear Sheila Mackay,
Thank you for showing me Colin Donati's poem.
He's done a difficult thing,
In my opinion,
And really brought it off.
The whole poem is
A steely cat's cradle —
A little model of the bridge
And very alive with all the stresses and weather
And full of interesting details.
And something else important —

It's very likeable.
What a good thing
I didn't attempt it!
He also seems to know what
He's talking about.
Another big plus. And
I surely do think
You'll have to go a long way
To find a better one.

Sincerely
Ted Hughes

BEGORRAH, or something like that, but it seems that the really professional player of the spoons doesn't just go and raid the cutlery drawer before clicking and banging the implements on his palm, his trousers, the top of his head etc.

A book called *Ireland's Musical Instrument Makers*, from Salmon Publishing, in Galway, was reviewed in *Cencrastus* magazine. It reveals that there is a full-time maker of musical spoons, and that spoon-playing has its own mythology.

'Spoons players are to be admired for their resourcefulness. Should their instruments happen to be mislaid or stolen, they will resort to clicking two bottles together or rattling a handful of loose change.

'Unhappily, decimal coinage has not got the same satisfying ring as the old copper pennies . . . '

WITH Dublin in the grip of Culture Year, the name game was at full stretch. The Anna Livia fountain in O'Connell Street was rechristened 'The Floozie in the Jacuzzi', and worse was to follow.

The Molly Malone statue in Grafton Street became 'The Tart with the Cart', the bronze group of women in Liffey Street became 'The Hags with the Bags'; and the newly-renovated government buildings in Merrion Street, named after the *taoiseach* Charles Haughey, became 'Château Charlemagne' (except that his critics spelled it 'Charlie-mange').

AN ITALIAN company called Ballad Opera dei Cantastorie was touring Britain and Ireland with its production of *Pinocchio*. So that English-speaking audiences were fully aware of where they were at, the following explanation was handed out at the theatre door:

'To show at an European public our own way of performit. We are Italians (in our good or bad culture) and we always did show ourselves in making a mere Italian theatre we will propose this vision:

'A thatrical stage space of no determinate deepness, stretchy in the front stage, which compact the public. In front of the public there will be room only for an actor, who will act and go away then another one will come, and others and many others will, all of them acting like the first one, after a short time. In different points of this immaginary thatrical space, the actors will mowe less visibly because they are far, and seem to become "dark forms" when suddenly a light will call them to the direct contact with the public, performing a costant evolution of many kinds, between actors and public.

'And from this acting will burst the Chorus walking in front of our eyes. With the Chorus we are (like we said in advance) at the "Italian Theatre". And now we are at the Greek Heritage, with them here is our "Italian Theatre". A drum, a filharmonic, a clarinet, a guitar, Pinocchio, Arlecchino, Pulcinella, Colombina, the ministrals, the ballad singers (Cantastorie), the buffons, the clowns, saltimbanchi, ecc . . . '

Er, don't call us.

EVERYBODY loves a festival. Or do they? There's more than one way of interpreting this announcement:

A thanksgiving ceremony to mark the end of Stockbridge Festival will take place on Sunday July 28 at 4.30pm.

BAD luck for Timothy Clifford, the controversial director of the Scottish National Galleries. *Harpers & Queen* magazine decided to interview his daughter on the incredibly boring subject of the London 'season'. We quote, with raised eyebrows:

'The mothers may concede that social mobility is here to stay, but their daughters wonder how open to change they really are. Pandora Clifford, whose father is director of the National Gallery of Scotland and a former debs' delight, took her boyfriend to parties, but she suspects her mother was hoping the Season would end the liaison.

'He isn't suitable. He has the wrong sort of family background and a bit of a

Scottish accent; he doesn't automatically call my father "sir". He goes to Merchiston, which is a public school, but a secondary one. My mother thinks why on earth couldn't I have chosen someone from Eton?'

It seems that to Pandora, the absolute nadir of the 'season' was the Queen Charlotte's Ball — 'the ultimate in *nouveau riche*'. Her father didn't seem to enjoy it either. 'Dad sat on a table with a load of second-hand car dealers, and he's not remotely interested in that sort of thing,' she told *Harper's & Queen*. Good grief.

FOR all of its working-class pretensions, the 7:84 Theatre Company is not above a spot of ostentation. When the company was presented with a new van by a Glasgow motor dealership, most people didn't notice that along with the vehicle came that tiresome yuppie status-symbol, a 'personalised' number plate:

LIFE on the boards is full of variety. Actor Robin Begg appeared in Tom McGrath's *Border Warfare* in Glasgow, not only as Sir William Wallace but also as Bonnie Prince Charlie; so it probably came as no surprise to him when he had a phone call from the Adam Smith Centre in Kirkcaldy, asking if he'd like to audition for *Mother Goose*.

'*Mother Goose*?' he queried.

'That's right. The musical,' said the voice. 'We're doing it in May.'

Pantomime in the spring sounded a little odd; but why not, if it brought in the crowds? So Begg prepared a jolly thigh-slapping audition piece and presented himself at Kirkcaldy. There, he slapped his thigh resoundingly before a slightly poker-faced audition panel.

When he was finished, he asked cheerfully: 'Who's playing the goose?'

'Goose?' echoed the panel.

'You know — *Mother Goose*,' returned Begg.

'No, no,' shrieked the selectors. 'What we're doing is *Irma La Douce*!'

PREPARING for European Cultural Capitalisation, one Glasgow pub specialising in beer from all over Britain started listing its available brews on a blackboard bearing the legend 'Ale la Carte'.

THE old catgut violin strings of yore, sounding true but liable to go twang . . . where are they now? Lost in translation, it seems, to judge by this passage from the wrapper of a modern violin-string, made in Venice:

> **Thanks to this type of metal strings, it has been possible to achieve both the switness of sound and the softness, to feel that one can recall the bowel strings of the past, but this type far better than the latter owing to the promptness in emission and the ready and stable tuning.**

But have catgut strings disappeared entirely? We heard of a domestic moggie expressing doubts on this one. A notice in a Portpatrick shop window read: 'Lost — our cat. Never been away from home before. Very skeptical circumstances.'

AN enthusiastic concert-goer, who attended three orchestral performances at the Usher Hall, discovered something rather interesting. At the first two concerts, programmes were being sold for 75p: at the third, the programme cost £1. He asked a steward why so. Answer: 'There have been huge queues at the programme sellers. Everyone seemed to be proferring pound notes, and the sellers quickly ran out of change.' Neat solution, no?

BROWSERS at Ian Thompson's exhibition *The Blind and the Naked* came away startled by the artist's imagery. But they hadn't seen nothing yet; for he had some paintings at home in Leith which weren't on show.

Among them were two on the theme of the Immaculate Conception, innocuously called *Painting 1* and *Painting 2*. Both show a couple displaying what might politely be termed the essential pre-conditions for reproduction of the species. However, because of the theme of these works, the male's participation is unnecessary, and he is wearing an expression of acute disgust.

After these works were completed, however, the artist painted large black stars over the males' naughty bits. Why so?

Ian's wife Barbara explained that this happened just before the artist's mother was dropping in for a visit. 'When she'd called round previously to see some of his paintings she just about had a fit. There was a friend with her bringing a young son and, well, she ended up apologising to him.'

So the black stars appeared mysteriously on the painting just in time.

It's probably just as well that Michelangelo's mum didn't call in to see how he was getting on in the Sistine Chapel.

HERE is an interesting new definition, overheard at the tenth anniversary of Jeddart Collogue, held by the Lowland & Border Pipers' Society in Jedburgh Town Hall:

'Bagpipes have been described as the missing link between noise and music.'

DEVOTEES of Sir Walter Scott — the man, the tradition, the image — will no doubt be aware of a publicity leaflet produced to attract visitors to Abbotsford, the house in the Borders where he lived and worked in the early 19th century. It tells us: 'Sir Walter Scott purchased the Cartley Hall farmhouse on the banks of the Tweed in 1812. Together with his family and servants, he moved into the farm which he renamed Abbotsford.'

But — aha — is this part of the continuing effort to gloss over the murky truth? Most modern publications refer to the old farmhouse as 'Cartley Hole' rather than 'Cartley Hall'. The official guide to Abbotsford modifies this to 'Cartleyhole'.

The truth — as borne out by Lockhart and other biographers — is that it bore none of these names. It was actually called 'Clarty Hole' (*clarty*, adj, dirty, muddy, sticky — *Concise Scots Dictionary*) and earned this unattractive title through the presence of a particularly disgusting duckpond in front of the house.

Within an hour of gaining possession of the property, Scott — with his instinct for the apt and his ear for the mellifluous — changed its name to Abbotsford. This was based on the presence of a nearby ford where the Gala Water joins the Tweed, and the fact that the lands had once belonged to the Abbey of Melrose.

Later he wrote to his brother-in-law: 'We are not a little proud of being greeted as laird and lady of Abbotsford.' Certainly, 'Laird of Clarty Hole' would not have had the same ring.

AN IRRESISTIBLE offer. The newsletter of the Clydesdale Arts Network warned that Greenhill Farmhouse Museum, near Biggar, had been putting on displays of 'sinning and weaving'.

HELIUM-FILLED balloons, given to children at various Edinburgh events, turned out to be something of a security nightmare. This is what happened at the Muppets and Magic exhibition in the City Art Centre:

After visiting the exhibition, the child with attendant balloon is taken by the parents to the Art Centre Café. The balloon escapes from the child's grasp and drifts up to the ceiling. The tearful child leaves, balloonless. Much later — usually at something like 3 a.m. — the balloon has lost enough gas to start sinking downwards . . . setting off the building's infra-red anti-burglar sensors and alerting security staff. The security men come at the run, full of adrenalin — to find themselves arresting a sadly-wrinkled balloon.

This led to security panics at the Museum of Childhood and the Brass-Rubbing Centre. Children were advised to tie the pesky balloons to a finger. And staff at the Art Centre Café had a new duty to do before they locked up: capturing escaped balloons with a piece of sticky tape attached to a long pole. That's progress.

THIS sort of thing shouldn't be encouraged. But a reader from Ayr, deep in Rabbie Burns country, responded to news that Dumfries Labour Party planned a McGonagall Supper. 'They are using one poet to beat the other with,' she said disapprovingly, before adding in sort of verse:

I hope it will be remembered in the town
for a very long time with a frown
That the people drinking and laughing at the poet William McGonagall and putting him down
And causing several of their members to cough and splutter by their remarks in the hall
Could never at any time in their lives have written any kind of poem at all

William himself could hardly have put it worse.

THE Master of Vatican Music — the Pope's organist — wanted to attend his first Burns Supper and was invited along by Edinburgh Robert Burns Club. There, the master of ceremonies was none other than the late Revd Alan Cameron, one-time Grand Master of the Orange Order in Scotland and better known as a piping busker of Princes Street.

The esteemed visitor, Dr Alberto Massimo, *organista e direttore d'orchestra*, enjoyed himself thoroughly and even won a bottle of whisky in the raffle. He was so impressed by Cameron's bagpipe rendering of the Italian national anthem that he sprang up and stood to attention.

(Cameron told the Diary that he played *The Sash* afterwards 'to balance things up'.)

Then Cameron — the last man to lead an Orange march on horseback — was invited to take his pipes across to the Vatican. He went too.

ANOTHER massive money-saving achievement from the Scottish Arts Council, moving into new premises at Manor Place, Edinburgh.

The new greenish curtains decorating the reception area seemed to have been specially made, with the SAC logo woven into the design: but in fact, a helpful interior designer found a curtain material which would resemble the logo if it was hung upside down. So there you are.

WE discovered a new cult-figure in Jerzy Maksymiuk, the Polish conductor and Harpo Marx lookalike, who took charge of the BBC Scottish Symphony Orchestra while also musical director of the renowned Polish Chamber Orchestra.

Some of the Scottish players met a few of their Polish counterparts, an ideal opportunity to 'swap Jerzys' as it were. 'He's a great guy,' said one of the Glasgow-based musicians, 'but his English is hell. Sometimes we have a real job making out what he's saying to us.'

'Don't worry,' said one of the Poles cheerfully. 'We don't understand him either.'

Maksymiuk's extravagant, not to say frenetic style amazed some of his musicians in Queen Margaret Drive, and won him the nickname 'Maximusic'.

One of the players explained that the system really works. 'Jerzy doesn't actually need to give us a beat. When his braces come undone and his trousers fall down, we play the final chord.'

IT was no mean honour for the championship-winning Desford Colliery Band (which no longer has a colliery) to be taken to Moscow to play at the British-Soviet Trade Fair.

The band gave performances at the Sovin Centre and other venues — but the absolute feather in the Desford cap was the invitation to play at the Moscow Conservatoire, a centre of musical excellence with an auditorium capable of seating 1,800 people.

A vehicle had to be sent to take the band's instruments to the concert hall. When it arrived, it turned out to be a lorry with the Russian word for 'Rubbish' painted on the side. The only available transport had been found at the city's department of waste management.

THE Wicked Ladies theatre company is now very much aware of the sod's law principle which states that if anything can go wrong, it will.

The Ladies were rehearsing in Glasgow's Queen Street Club for the production of *The Third Tenant* and which calls for a shot to be fired. In this case, the explosion was so deafening that a horse outside, with a policewoman on board, nearly bolted in panic. At the same time, somebody inside the building called in the law.

The Wicked Ladies were let off with a laugh, and a warning.

ONE of the highlights of the Edinburgh Folk Festival's farewell ceilidh was a sort of Houdini act, witnessed by only a handful of revellers. Two burly folkies had apparently paid for their tickets and strolled into the venue, Edinburgh University's Teviot Row Union, carrying a bulky sports-bag between them. This they set gently down on the floor in the bar.

Bystanders were surprised, to say nothing of alarmed, to notice the bag moving. 'There's something alive in there,' remarked one. He was invited not to *fash himself*.

At a suitable moment, the bag was unzipped and out stepped a fairly large man. He was taken to a shady corner where he could enjoy the ceilidh without being noticed, and his friends continued to supply his needs from the bar.

It turned out that this was a folk follower who had been ejected from a previous event at the Festival for over-enthusiasm, and was banned from subsequent concerts. The final ceilidh, however, was something he was determined not to miss . . .

NEWS from the often-bewildering world of theatre. The Traverse Studio in Edinburgh staged the premiere of Brendan Nash's show *2–4–6–8, Is Your Husband Really Straight?* This, the advance publicity told us seriously, 'follows Nash's previous success with *Quick Phyllis, Grab a Dyke and Dance Your Way Out. It's a Raid* which toured nationally in 1988 delighting audiences and "pretend families" wherever it went.'

GAELIC intrigue surrounded the first competitive appearance of the Stornoway Masonic Choir, whose existence became known only when the Mod programme was printed. A local observer said that the choir had been a well-guarded secret, but added, 'Handshakes with the judges are prohibited.'

However, Mod historians will recall something of a precedent. At the first Mod in 1892, the leading poet Mary MacPherson ('Great Mary of the Songs') shook hands with an adjudicator before launching into her performance. Alas, she was unplaced. Our Mod observer feels that she probably didn't know the right handshake.

M E D I A

TRICKY one for the Radio Forth celeb whose early morning task is to fly over Edinburgh and advise motorists that the roads are blocked, as usual. One day the flying road-traffic guide didn't manage to get into his usual hovering situation until 8.20 a.m. Unfortunately, he'd been stuck in a traffic jam while trying to make his way to the airport.

APRIL FOOL spoofs have a terrible habit of becoming permanent, and the case is proved with the statutory leg-pull in the *East Kilbride News*. It told of an exciting experiment in which the National Engineering Laboratory and Scandinavian scientists were conducting a joint experiment in heat loss, applying lessons from space-shuttle technology to local schoolchildren.

And so (grinds the tale) East Kilbride kids would wear wristbands made of 'solar foil' which would reflect body heat. Classroom ceilings would be covered in the foil, to diminish the effect of rising hot air.

The clues in the story were, however, fairly numerous. It referred to the Chancellor's *April fuel* rises; to a *Dr A. V. Alaf* of *Stavanger Technical University for Professional Inventors and Developers* (work out the acronym); and to a *Professor Colm E. Dian* (say it quickly).

Alas, none of this was twigged by the Glasgow *Evening Times*, which duly rewrote the story four days later under the headline 'Lessons in Heat Saving'. A lesson, in fact, in something else altogether.

IN the freight business, refrigerated semi-trailers are apparently known as 'reefers' for short. A police raid on one of these vehicles in north London turned up a quantity of drugs. Which gave a sub-editor on *Motor Transport* magazine a chance to write the droll headline he'd always dreamed of:

Cannabis found in reefer

A CERTAIN Steve Ridinger from Irvine, California, is the first person in the world known to have shot himself in the foot with the ubiquitous fax machine.

As president of a fax supply company, he was one of the few Americans not incensed when this new development in communications was 'discovered' by the junk-mail industry. In Connecticut, however, so many people were disgusted by the constant stream of unsolicited promotional material through their machines that state legislation seeking to outlaw this practice was awaiting the Governor's signature.

This was when Steve Ridinger swung into action. He organised a mass lobby by the industry, urging the Governor to veto the measure. Naturally, everyone sent their protests by fax. The Governor was so annoyed to find his fax machine clogged up with the protests that he signed the Bill at the toot . . .

RECORDING ethnic music for radio can be like wandering into a minefield. BBC Radio Scotland staff, working on an item for a Radio 2 Arts programme, decided to send a sound engineer to Findhorn to record somebody playing a didgeridoo. Well, why not? It makes a change from the bagpipes.

The didgeridoo, of course, is a wind instrument perfected (if that is the word) by Australian aborigines. The sound it makes is a sort of low groan punctuated by burbles and soft honks.

The engineer duly recorded one Craig Gibsone at his labours and sent the tape to Edinburgh.

Here we must pause for some technical gen. Sometimes, tapes are stored on a spool back to front (i.e. 'tail out') and sometimes they arrive the right way round ('head out'). A little coloured sticker should be attached to the tape to indicate which procedure is being followed. But the didgeridoo tape had no sticker.

Then followed a hour or two of pure torture as the programme people played this tape backwards and forwards repeatedly in an attempt to decide which way it should run.

To their utter consternation, it didn't seem to make a lot of difference. The sound of a didgeridoo played backwards is remarkably similar to the sound of a didgeridoo played forwards. But, of course, an expert would be able to tell, so they had to get the thing right.

They got their recording man on the phone and forced him to listen to this mournful sound, played in both directions. They even concentrated on the sound of the performer filling his lungs for the next groan — on the grounds that a sharp intake of breath, played backwards, might sound like a sharp expulsion of breath.

A decision was finally agreed upon. It was all right on the night. They think.

WHAT was happening at BBC Scotland? Rampant nepotism? Clannishness? A rash of pseudonyms? A reader sent us a cutting from *Radio Times* showing that hot on the heels of a programme produced by David Jackson Young came one produced by Bruce Young. It's a story by Douglas Young, read by Paul Young.

This was almost as confusing as a certain rugby score. In the game between Anglo-Scots Under-21s and South Under-21s, the score (naturally) was 21–21. Try reading it aloud.

JOURNALISTS are inclined to be a bit paranoid about telephones, convinced that the Special Branch spends its time eavesdropping on their exclusives. The paranoia was heightened for hacks planning to descend on Harrogate for a CBI conference, when they discovered the name of the British Telecom man who would organise their communications. Step forward Mr Tony Tapper.

IN polite society, there are numerous ways of showing displeasure with a fellow human being. These range from *cutting one dead* (i.e., pretending not to notice one) to *the elegant riposte* (i.e., dismissing one with a devastating, off-the-cuff witticism).

However, the Diary heard of an entirely new tactic, tried out for the first time at a festive season encounter where Scottish Television's Edinburgh staff were host to various important local figures at its Gateway Studios.

Among the guests were certain Edinburgh City councillors, and among the hosts was telly-journo Nick Radcliffe, a man well known for his sartorial impeccability even when turning out to cover such events as a fire in a plastics factory.

For this social affair, Mr Radcliffe was smartly be-suited, with a colour-co-ordinated handkerchief in his breast pocket. But there came a moment when he was engaged in lively conversation with a councillor, whom we shall refrain from naming for reasons too complex to go into here. The councillor's response at one point in their discussion was to remove the handkerchief from Mr Radcliffe's pocket, blow his nose in it, and hand it back.

Those who witnessed this tactic were stunned by its simple effectiveness. Mr Radcliffe, for his part, was later heard bemoaning the ravaging of his hanky which (he pointed out) was of 'hand-rolled silk'.

We do not believe, however, that this highly original social manoeuvre is likely to enter the various handbooks on how to conduct oneself in the nation's drawing-rooms.

CAMEL cigarettes, whose products sell briskly in South Africa, had something of a setback with their advertising campaign there.

Their theme — of a healthy outdoor man doing healthy outdoor things against a dramatic background of mountains and crystal clear rivers — was pushed heavily in magazines and even through giant hoardings on the motorways.

Unfortunately they had to start again. The healthy outdoor man died of lung cancer.

ONLY a sense of humour makes the Silly Season tolerable for journos. We heard of a colleague making a routine call to an ambulance station, who was asked:

'Did you hear about the accident at the Gogar roundabout?'

'No'. (Reaches for pen and notebook.)

'It was a collision between a prison van and a cement lorry.'

'Really?' (Scribble, scribble.)

'Yes. The police are looking for six hardened criminals.'

'Oh very funny.' Sound of pen being thrown down. End of call.

HEADLINE of the century from the venerable *Dumfries & Galloway Standard*, which was celebrating a major anniversary of Maxwellton Bowling Club. Somewhat puzzlingly, it read: '1890 to 1990: A Decade of Success'.

HAND-ROLLED Havana tobacco can usually be found, burning aromatically, at those glittering events where the advertising industry likes to congratulate itself by distributing trophies after a substantial dinner. Such an event was the Design & Art Direction Awards ('the advertising Oscars') at London's Grosvenor House Hotel, where the Edinburgh-based Marr Associates got a silver award for a press advertisement.

And naturally, the Havanas came out for the occasion. The agency's MD, Colin Marr, sported a Graf Zeppelin of a smoke while his individual winners, Will Taylor and Tim Robertson, also displayed cigars (probably slightly smaller, we'd guess).

From this trio, however, not a whiff of expensive pungency drifted. Not a match was struck all night, until their neighbours began to burn instead — with curiosity. Was this the mythical Scottish parsimony at work?

It turned out, however, that the cigars were staying unlit in deference to the client for whom they'd crafted the winning ad: ASH, aka Action on Smoking and Health.

AN unexpected controversy over Santa Claus's nationality erupted sourly in London PR circles. Apparently, the idea that St Nicholas was a Turkish bishop 1,500 years ago was first floated in *PR Week* magazine, and drew a stinging riposte from a practitioner named Kevorkian.

Impossible, he says. There was no Turkey 1,500 years ago. When the Turks did emerge, they were never Christian. He concludes: 'I know Saatchi & Saatchi is being paid £3.5 million to get Turkey into Europe, but to try to do so by claiming that St Nicholas was a Turk is really a bit much . . . '

WE all know that the Shetland island of Unst is a bit distant from almost anywhere. This must be why Shetland's education department seemed to be seeking someone to teach a rather unusual subject to the 108 pupils at Baltasound Junior High School:

TEACHER OF ART REMOTENESS

Payment: £978 per annum.

The money didn't seem all that good either. All was explained, however, when the ad appeared elsewhere with a spot of judicious punctuation:

TEACHER OF ART

REMOTENESS PAYMENT: £978 PER ANNUM

WHY throw away a good advertising slogan that has worked in the past?

Before British Leyland's trucks division was sold off to the Dutch-based company, DAF, it operated under the memorable catchphrase 'the new driving force'.

One of British Leyland's former public relations men later started working as a PR consultant to Lothian & Edinburgh Enterprise Ltd (LEEL for short).

This local enterprise company — then produced a glossy report whose cover read: 'Introducing The New Driving Force'.

Recycling lives, it seems.

THE *Daily Record* went to considerable lengths to obtain pictures of Jason, the 18-year-old son of Manchester United manager Alex Ferguson, working in a Romanian orphanage. In fact, they went to greater lengths than they bargained for.

A photographer was dispatched from Glasgow to meet up with a Reuter's correspondent in Romania. But on his arrival there was no sign of her. He phoned back to base. 'She's not here,' he reported.

Funny: the arrangements were confirmed. She would meet the plane at Bucharest Airport. 'What d'ye mean, Bucharest,' said the pained lensman. 'You've sent me to Budapest.'

THE citizens' choo-choo charter got off to a rather bad start before it had even pulled out of the political station.

We heard of the strange experiences of a BBC Scotland reporter, with film team, who wanted to chronicle the happy lifestyle of a typical Edinburgh-Glasgow commuter and his dependence on the daily lottery of Waverley-Queen Street rail travel.

A suitable subject was duly identified and the filming project cleared with the BR press office. But as the commuter waited to achieve immortality via the 8 a.m. Edinburgh-Glasgow train, word came that the service had been cancelled: shortage of rolling stock.

Wonderful: so it had to be the next train. As the all-seeing eye of television prowled the coaches of the train, looking for a suitable picture, it came across a gent in the First Class section, wearing a British Rail tie. Aha, the veritable horse's mouth: perhaps it would care to speak?

But the luckless gentleman naturally did not think this was the appropriate moment for him to talk on behalf of the railways.

In fact, he was travelling to begin the first day in his new job at the BR press office in Glasgow. And he was going to be late.

And his previous job? Well, he'd been with the Department of Transport helping to work out the terms of the citizens' charter — you know, the thing that promises compensation for late or cancelled services.

Oh dear. But thanks anyway.

A THOROUGHLY charming piece of evidence was offered in a drinks-driving case against *Daily Mail* gossip columnist Nigel Dempster, which was dismissed at Horseferry Road Magistrates Court in London. After he'd been arrested, Dempster apparently asked if he could use the police station telephone to phone his paper with copy for his column.

His counsel asked whether Dempster appeared competent enough to do this, in spite of the allegation that he had been drinking. The police constable's reply was something of a classic. 'So far as I know sir, by reporters' standards, he was doing all right.'

THERE are unexpected dangers for poll tax refuseniks, we hear. One such was Lothian regional councillor Neil Lindsay, who was photographed burning his community charge payment book over a brazier. The photographers demanded so many re-takes that all the hairs were singed from Lindsay's forearm. Another snag was that through a shortage of combustibles, the fire had to be started with copies of *Militant*.

ONE sure sign that your political star is rising is that the BBC Pronunciation Unit in London starts to make discreet inquiries about you. Inevitably, this happened to the Labour chairman in Scotland, Mark Lazarowicz, who threw BBC current affairs johnnies into confusion merely by appearing on a conference platform at Dunoon.

The pronunciation specialists started off by checking with Labour's London HQ, where the first response was 'Who's he?' Later, after a hunt through the files, they came back with a definitive 'Sorry, we don't know anyone of that name.'

The unit was left to forage for Lazarowicz insights at the BBC's various branch offices in Scotland where, no doubt, they discovered everyone pronounces the name a different way.

STIRLING District Council's writer-in-residence, Jim Wilson, was often asked some highly technical questions by the area's aspiring authors.

But one question that was put to him left him completely stuck for a suitable explanation: 'Why does *True Romances* magazine have a fiction editor?'

THE advertising business is no place for the faint-hearted, especially when there are Australians on the horizon. The London-based director of the Australian Tourist Commission wrote to *Marketing Week* to quash a rumour that he would soon be looking for a new agency to handle his plum account. How did he learn about the rumour? Simply that unsolicited promotional material from ambitious agencies started to form a mountain on his doormat.

'As a result,' he said, 'the material we have received over the past week from agencies is creating a problem for our rubbish removers. Enough is enough . . . Don't call us, we'll call you.' Seems clear enough.

HEADLINES — we love 'em. They're a contemporary art form, and here are some of our collectables:

• From the *Ayrshire Leader*: 'CAMMY FOR SAMMY BUT HAMMY JAMMY'. This requires a little explanation. Ayr United had secured the services of goalkeeper Cammy Duncan from Partick Thistle in exchange for a midfield player, Sammy Johnston. Nevertheless, in the goalkeeper's first game for Ayr at Somerset Park, the team went down 1–2 to Hamilton Accies. Naturally, the *Leader's* sportswriter thought the visitors were lucky. Got it?

• An interesting stretch of the imagination from the *Deeside Piper*. The tale concerned an artificial pond installed without planning permission. The headline: 'LUMPHANAN POND IN HOT WATER'.

• Double-take headline from the *John o' Groats Journal*: 'SURFERS CAUSE PROBLEMS ON PRIVATE ROAD'. Beg pardon? The explanation: road maintenance problems were being caused by the carloads of surfers on their way to a Thurso beach. Aha.

• From the Zimbabwe *Weekend Gazette*: 'MUNYORO CHALLENGES BANANA'. But the story — concerning the former president, Prof Canaan Banana — was even more interesting; for Gibson Munyoro MP was commenting on Banana's plans for 'a revised version of the Bible'.

He wished to remind the professor that it was God who made him first president of Zimbabwe, although some might say it was the leader of ZANU (PF), Robert Mugabe, who was responsible. Then there was the suggestion by the Member for Mbare East that President Mugabe was 'the only other son of God, putting him on a par with Jesus Christ'. This allegation had since been withdrawn.

Mr Munyoro now felt that Professor Banana's appointment had been a blend of divine and political inspiration, and there the matter rested.

THE *Orcadian* must have been a bit short on commas, quotation marks and other essentials for punctuation when it was listing the events for the Orkney Science Festival. Thus its devotees were promised the following absolutely irresistible attractions.

'The Utter Impossibility of Intelligent Life in Kirkwall.'

'Why Hasn't Scotland Exploded in Stromness?'

'Pictish Telecommunications in Papa Westray.'

'Mammal Communication by Smell in Kirkwall.'

'The True Story of Rudolph Hess in Stromness.'

'The Secret Life of John Logie Baird in the Hope.'

EMBARRASSING moment? How about this: BBC Scotland radio reporter Ninian Reid was interviewing all comers at an exhibition in Huntly House Museum devoted to 200 years of hairstyling in the City of Edinburgh. He wondered about wigs, and he was introduced to wigmaker George Theurer of A & A Hair Studio.

'Well,' said the intrepid reporter, with the tape-recorder capturing all, 'you certainly still have all of your hair.' At this, he tugged Theurer's thatch which stayed firmly in place. 'Actually you're wrong there,' said the expert, lifting off his wig from the back.

Poor Reid dissolved into profuse apologies, but the wig-man was unfazed. 'It's very reassuring when something like that happens,' he told the Diary. 'Modern hairpieces don't come off unless you want them to. I know that they are a source of humour to many people — but they are very serious to us, I assure you.'

There had been no need for the radio reporter to apologise, he declared. 'It was like apologising to a comedian for laughing at his jokes.'

FOR Julian Barnes, author of *A History of the World in 10½ Chapters*, it was a moment to be savoured. In Edinburgh for the Book Festival, he had been spirited along the road to Waterstone's bookshop to sign copies for his adoring readers.

While engaged in this pleasant duty, he was approached by a woman bearing a copy of his tome. And to whom, he inquired politely, should it be dedicated?

'To Rupert,' said Mrs Anna Murdoch, for indeed it was she.

Pause. 'I'm not sure he would appreciate it,' said Barnes. 'He once fired me from *The Times*.'

The reply was a classic. 'I'm sure it was nothing personal.'

HERE is a telling item from Edinburgh Film Festival's daily information sheet, colourfully entitled *Sex, Lies and Daily News*: 'Unless guests refrain from removing the cutlery from the Press Room, they might be forced to eat with their fingers in future.'

A SURREAL controversy about golliwogs in Peebles drew BBC radio reporter Ninian Reid to the Borders to seek local opinion. Armed with his tape-recorder, he went around the houses to ask local residents their views on the traditional Beltane parade, for which schoolchildren used to dress up as gollies in a time-honoured but nowadays rather dubious ritual.

He found himself knocking on doors in a sheltered-housing complex — where one resident looked at him doubtfully and phoned the police. In due course, the police were in touch with the BBC, trying to establish whether there had been somebody attempting to masquerade as a radio journalist.

This must have been rather trying for poor Ninian Reid; for he also happens to be a member of that area's Tweeddale Crime Prevention Panel! But at least he had the satisfaction of knowing that the panel's message about *suspicious-looking persons* was getting through.

CLEARLY, the best DIY tips come from people with personal experience. This useful piece of advice, from a women's magazine, might not have been taken so seriously were it not for the name of the contributor:

■ When applying liquid shading on a greenhouse, whiten the inside of the roof panes rather than the outside. This makes the job easier, especially if you are not very tall.

Mrs J Small,
Plymouth, Devon

FOR switched-on coverage of the arts in Scotland, what could be better than the weekly TV programme succintly called *NB*, on Scottish. They were very anxious to do something about an exhibition of paintings by Stanley Spencer, one of Britain's foremost 20th-century artists, appearing at the Kelvingrove Gallery in Glasgow. So somebody phoned the gallery. A curator was stunned when asked if the artist was available for a recorded interview.

The answer was in the negative. Spencer (1891-1959) wasn't talking to the *meeja* any more — under any circumstances.

AFTER three years as a building site, BBC Scotland's Edinburgh headquarters welcomed its lads and lassies back again. The various departments moved in to the refurbished Queen Street offices from cramped quarters round the corner and the new studios were expected to be going full blast a week later.

One of the problems of BBC Scotland's temporary arrangement in Thistle Street was that there was no canteen. In a laudable bid to make amends, BBC managers ensured that the canteen at Queen Street was the first space to be ready — full of gleaming hotplates and shiny new furniture.

It appeared however, that there was no canteen staff. Did somebody forget to advertise?

THIS was the sorry tale of an Edinburgh advertising man, a reader of *Scotland on Sunday*. At least, he was trying to be a reader of *Scotland on Sunday*.

What happened two weeks before was that the delivery boy popped the *Sunday Post* through his letterbox. Our hero was not amused, leaped into his car and drove down to the newsagent's. 'Terribly sorry,' said the newsagent, taking the *Post* and giving him an *SoS* in exchange. One week later, the same thing happened. 'Terribly sorry', said the newsagent, and the same transaction was courteously negotiated.

But the following Sunday it happened again. By that time the victim was incandescent. He walked to the head of a long Sunday-morning queue to make his complaint, and the newsagent was quite puzzled. 'What did you say your name was?' he inquired, consulting his order book. Then he said: 'We don't actually deliver papers to you, sir.'

We draw a veil over the advertising man's feelings. He had been complaining to the wrong newsagent. Ha.

REDUNDANCY is no joke, of course. But when a local timber yard had to lay off six of its people, a company spokesman told the *Berwick Advertiser* that the job losses were 'across the board'.

AFICIONADOS of well-timed advertising slots would appreciate the commercial break during ITV's *World in Action* programme on the Birmingham Six. The sales pitch was: 'It's never too early to phone a solicitor . . . '

HERE'S the sort of apology that might be appreciated by ladies and gentlemen of the cloth. The *Ross-shire Journal* confessed that, in reporting appointments to Ross, Cromarty & Skye local health council, it inadvertently styled a Mr Paterson of Tain 'the Rev.'. The paper said: 'We regret any inconvenience this may have caused Mr Paterson' — and presumably, only a Highland minister can know precisely what this means.

FROM the *East Lothian Courier*, there was news with serious implications for the Gregorian calendar:

The May Ball has been postponed to June 16.

THE committee members of Melness Gaelic Féis in north Sutherland were disconcerted to find the local media announcing a rather saucier event than they had in mind. In spite of the organisers' extreme care to include the acute accent when publicising their entertainment, newspapers in the north tended to leave it out.

As anyone with recourse to Dwelly's Gaelic dictionary will be aware, the word *feis* means something else. As Mr Edward Dwelly puts it in his sternly moral manner, it indicates 'carnal intercourse'. This could attract audiences of a kind the committee did not particularly seek: so they wished to point out that the first evening session — billed as 'Activities: Games, Videos etc' — would be of a strictly moral nature.

The fact that the Melness féis is largely taking place 18 miles away in another village, Bettyhill, is beyond the powers of any dictionary to explain.

THE term 'visual display unit', shortened to VDU, is with us to stay, according to the Datum Line column in *New Civil Engineer*. In the United States, however, these are known as 'visual display terminals' . . . the abbreviation for which 'is hated by journalists since it summarises the two things they fear most'. Very funny.

NORTHERNERS waited with amused interest to monitor the progress of the *Daily Record*'s circulation drive in the area. The paper published a map which confidently showed, a few miles north of Wick, a non-existent town named 'Caithness'. Diary readers were asking: how many copies will the imaginary residents of this burgh be ordering from their fictional newsagents?

READERS of the *'Scottish' Daily Express* were puzzled by the following entry in its television page:

11.5 GRASPING THE NETTLE.

The programme — a debate on Scottish self-government, chaired by

Kirsty Wark — was actually called *Grasping the Thistle*. But naturally everyone assumed it was a repeat of the doughty Kirsty's famous interview with the former Prime Minister, Mrs Thatcher.

RADIO 4's *Thought for the Day*, usually a very considered if not sober-sided slot, is an unlikely vehicle for a laugh. Thus listeners were startled over their toast and marmalade to hear Dr David Cook, of King's College, Cambridge, use the prog to deliver a rather good joke.

It ran like this: 'When President Bush went to heaven, he asked to see Moses. An emissary went off to find the Old Testament lad, and returned shaking his head. Moses wouldn't see the president. The last time he spoke to a bush, he spent 40 years in the wilderness . . . '

This sort of thing could liven up Sundays no end.

SPORT

HOW's this for the ultimate victory over the Auld Enemy. After England beat Scotland at Murrayfield in the Rugby World Cup semi-final, a woman from Kirkcaldy saw a group of five Englishmen pull out the celebratory bottles of whisky which they'd kept hidden for that moment. Well, naturally, she informed the nearest policeman didn't she? After the transgressors were arrested she left the ground, we hear, with a secret smile on her face.

NOW for the *real* World Cup. After England fans in Italy did their habitual riot act, a remarkable accolade for Scotland's Tartan Army came from (of all places) Shanghai. The *Xinmin Evening Post* had a reporter in Turin to watch Scotland's last throw of the dice against Brazil; but quite honestly, he found the Scots supporters more remarkable than the team. His report appeared under the headline:

优秀的球迷

This translates as 'Fine Football Fans'. What surprised the reporter was that although the Brazil game was decisive for Scotland (in other words, they were *oot*) the Scots supporters showed nothing but friendliness towards their Brazilian counterparts. After the game, the Scots fans shook hands with the Brazilians.

Even the Italian policemen were astonished by this happy docility. One officer said: 'If it had been the Italian team that went out, we don't know how many extra policemen would have to be brought in' (a slight calumny, as it later turned out).

The Chinese reporter did, however, get his facts in a twist when he asked: 'Why is there such a difference between Scottish and English fans, even though they belong to the same country?'

HUMBLE thanks to the readers who pointed out that in the previous item we printed a certain headline upside down. To end the confusion, this is what we should have said:

优秀的球迷

LUDICROUS quote from a football World Cup TV commentary. John Motson rounded off the tournament with: 'And there's Beckenbauer, standing in that upright position . . . '

Hib infection *The clinical indications explained which necessitate routine immunisation against Hib from October 1992*

CERTAIN Edinburgh football supporters weren't surprised to learn that the Department of Health was to introduce a vaccine to help them. According to Pulse, the Hib bacteria is particularly dangerous when it catches children under four.

As Easter Road regulars know, the Hib condition affects mainly boys. It can come on suddenly, often at night, and one symptom is a sore throat. Unfortunately, the vaccine wouldn't be available until the end of the season, but 'even one dose should provide some protection against Hib'. And about time too.

BEFORE Hearts chairman Wallace Mercer withdrew his takeover bid for Hibs, some Hibernian fans were nursing cases of acute pessimism. Indeed, one of them sent the Diary this memorable picture:

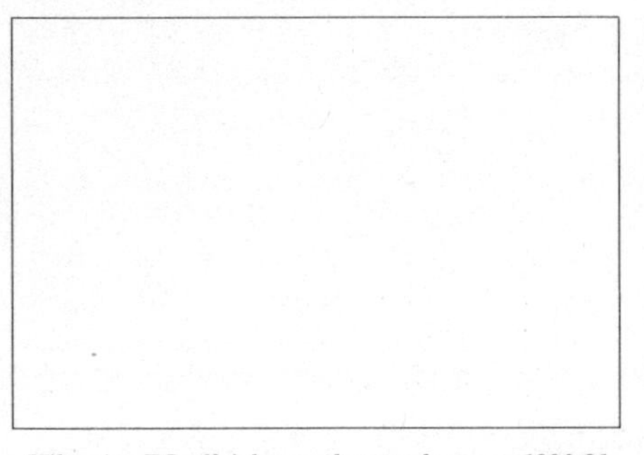

Hibernian FC official team photograph: season 1990-91

CELTIC'S interest in one Skol Cup campaign ended at the semi-final stage when they were beaten by Aberdeen 1–0 at Hampden. That was the match in which captain Roy Aitken was sent off by the referee, and in which Joe Miller was sent on as a substitute but withdrawn by his manager after 15 minutes. The Terracing Joke Factory went to work on this curious scenario, and the result goes like this:

'Have you heard that Celtic now has three Polish players? Dziekanowski, Aitkenoffsky, and Milleronandoffsky.'

ODD things seemed to be happening at Celtic FC. Hector Macmillan's play *The Sash* — examining the relationship between a Glasgow Orangeman and his son — was going on tour. 'It will be performed by a strong Celtic cast,' said the publicity blurb. We think we know what they meant.

THEN there's the *Sunday Telegraph*'s coverage of Celtic's home win against Falkirk. Their writer was much taken by the form of Gary Gillespie, a new Parkhead signing. 'He should bring some polished play to Parkhurst,' prophesied the writer, a little pessimistically.

TERRY BUTCHER, Chris Woods, Ian Durrant . . . the names of three Rangers players who had just appeared before the courts. Durrant's little peccadillo was to sing sectarian songs in a take-away food shop.

All this flitted through the mind of a Scottish regional councillor who attended one of those match-day hospitality events which are all the rage at Ibrox. Handed a copy of the Rangers Commercial Department 'Guide for Guests', his eyes bulged as he read:

'In keeping with the standards of dress maintained by Rangers Football Club, male guests are requested to wear a jacket and tie. The club would also request that all guests conduct themselves in a manner consistent with the fine traditions and reputation of Rangers Football Club.'

WHEN it was bidding for the Premier League Big Spender's Cup, Dunfermline Athletic put on show its newest signing, goalkeeper Andy Rhodes, bought from Oldham for £100,000.

As newspaper photographers set up their equipment at East End Park to record this shopping trip for posterity, manager Jim Leishman disclosed that he had spent nearly £500,000 in other close-season buys, and might have to shell out a further £300,000 to complete a deal for a Hungarian international.

Then it came time for the photographs. The photographers asked for the indispensable studio prop for such occasions, to wit, one football. East End Park was searched high and low, but a football couldn't be found.

We could only hope that Dunfermline would be able to afford one before training started in a couple of weeks' time.

THERE is sometimes more humour than talent in Edinburgh's amateur leagues (writes Our Touchline Troublemaker). He remembers a major bakery fielding a team called 'AC Milanda', and another club with a nod to Madrid calling itself 'Unreal Portobello'.

Football would be too serious a business without these lads.

FAMOUS GROUSE Scotch Whisky, the Rugby World Cup sponsor, collected some 'curious facts' about the game.

How about this one: 'In 1980 New Zealand were reputed to be improving their ball-handling skills by using house-bricks. This was at the behest of coach Eric Watson, who was unhappy with his three-quarters. So successful was this unorthodox ploy that the New Zealanders went on to beat arch-rivals Australia 26–10 and, in the process, earn the nickname, the All-Bricks.'

THE Diary asked readers for their curious facts. And got plenty . . .

- There was the match played by Edinburgh Borderers on a pitch seriously befouled by doggies' calling cards. Inevitably, the players' shorts were soon in a horrible state; and one second-row forward refused to stick his head between the front-row backsides until he'd borrowed his wife's 'Rainmate', which he tied on decorously over his scrum-cap.
- Then there was the Scotland-Wales game at Murrayfield, where the gathering crowd noticed that the Saltire was being flown at half-mast. As the teams ran out, it was announced that, sadly,

an SRU official had died that morning . . . followed by the response in a Welsh accent: 'Who got his ticket, then?'

• Denys Dobson, who played for England around 1902, had two claims to fame. He was the first man recorded as having been sent off for directing obscene language at a referee. But, on a note of finality, he is probably the only rugby player to have been killed by a rhinoceros, a fate which befell him when he emigrated to Nyasaland (now Malawi). He was reputed to have a weak hand-off.

SOME players will find this a tale with a familiar ring. It's an insight into the theory of collective responsibility and the magical workings of selection committees.

The former Irish wing, Tony O'Reilly, had been dropped from the squad for a match at Twickenham. Very discouraging. But he was invited to the after-match dinner, during which four of the five selectors came up to him separately to offer their commiserations.

Each one assured O'Reilly that — of course — he had voted to have him in the team. Thus the winger seems to be the only internationalist ever dropped after a vote by the selectors that was *at least* 4–1 in his favour.

NOT every rugby match sees three touch-downs before the kick-off. But the fixture between West Linton RC and Watsonian Juniors, played at the Peeblesshire club's rural home ground of Whitfield, was different in several ways.

The visiting players were warming up before the match with some physical jerks when a ewe wandered off the nearby hill, settled herself down amid the straining muscle-men, and promptly had triplets. There is nothing in the SRU handbook to cover that situation: but luckily the West Linton touch-judge, Billy Rutherford, was a shepherd and was able to cope with the situation and clean up the field of play.

Apart from that, it was not a memorable occasion for West Linton, up against a team which included no fewer than seven former Scottish Schools internationalists.

The home team went down by 16 points to 56 — 'like lambs to the slaughter', as one wag put it.

SCENE: The bar at Sutton Rugby Club, in a suburb of Dublin, where Suttonians are to play a team from Corstorphine.

The caretaker is trying to sweep away the debris of the previous night's disco, watched by a committee member who is standing Guinness-handed at the bar. The activity comes to a halt — again — as the broom falls apart.

'Typical,' says the observer with disgust. 'The head's come off five times. Now it's the bliddy handle.'

OH well — more rugby. Touching scenes of *après-rugger* fellowship were observed at Waverley Station, Edinburgh, following a Scotland-Wales encounter at Murrayfield. A mixed but good-natured crowd of supporters massed there seeking transport to various airts, and were entertained by a man with a trumpet.

His first offering was, unsurprisingly, *Flower of Scotland*, which drew raucous singing from the Scots fans. Then — even-handedly — he broke into *Bread of Heaven*, which drew a defiant response from the Welsh choristers. Finally he produced another number for the Welsh, *The Last Post*. For this, the emotional Taffies stood to attention and sadly, but with dignity, lowered their red-and-white scarves to the ground.

Scotland must have won that match.

THE Maoris may have perfected the posterior-flash as an eloquent form of insult: but the Scots are not far (as it were) behind. Following a rugby international in Dublin, letters erupted in the Irish press complaining about 'an unseemly display of kilt-lifting' by some Scottish fans.

One particularly outraged reader said: 'This needless display of vulgarity might lead people less kindly disposed than myself to Scotland and the Scots to wonder why Edward Longshanks and the Duke of Cumberland did not persevere.' So it's trousers from now on at Lansdowne Road, chaps.

MORE rugby news: With the French preparing for a raid on Murrayfield, there were some team problems to be sorted out. One newspaper reported this case of 'better late than never':

> Erbani's wife was due to leave hospital after giving birth. Jean Condom, the experienced Biarritz second row, was immediately called up.

A SCOTTISH rugby fan, living in Northampton, asked kin on this side of the Border to buy and send him the BBC video of Scotland's Grand Slam season. His mother duly went to a video shop and asked for the tape. As it was handed over, she noticed that it said 1984 on the cover. 'Isn't there a more recent one?' she inquired.

PRESS photographers sent overseas to Lansdowne Road, Dublin, to cover the Ireland v Scotland rugby international found this helpful note on their ground tickets: 'See reverse side for conditions regarding admission to the ground.'

Turning the tickets over, they weren't too surprised to find them entirely blank.

AND finally, rugbywise, BBC Radio Scotland reporter David Nisbet, a Geordie, somehow managed to acquire two centre-stand tickets for the World Cup final at Twickers. Then there was a phone call to the office, and colleagues saw him turn pale. It was his wife to tell him that their nine-month-old sprog had succeeded in tearing one of the billets in half. Panic calls to the SRU followed: would tickets be accepted at Twickers if they were in two pieces? They would: in fact, involuntarily torn tickets had been a bit of a problem throughout the series. So the England fan went to the match, and a fat lot of good it did him too.

THE most coveted post in Scottish medicine must be that of 'recorder' of the annual golf match between Edinburgh's Royal Colleges of Physicians and Surgeons.

Fellows of both formed the Royal Colleges Golf Club in 1890, and the match is played over the Luffness course, East Lothian, each May — with that year's official recorder taking notes of the day's often-surreal happenings and reporting hilariously on them at the annual dinner later in the year.

The club now has about 50 of these reports, and the *British Medical Journal* printed some extracts. It seems that the spectacle of 'drab Edinburgh bourgeoisie trudging round a golf course' has concealed some amazing feats of derring-do.

There are often comments on the golfers' dress, ranging from 'immaculate consulting attire' to 'a blue jersey borrowed from some obese fisherman'.

Surgeons, we learn, have a penchant for 'pus-coloured caps'. Another player sported a set of plus-fours with 'three zip fasteners which ensured that all things were possible, and in any direction'.

Some of the best one-liners recorded in past reports are from before 1950, largely because the golf trolley had not been invented and clubs had to be hefted by that droll and dogged breed, the caddy. This could prove useful for ego-deflation.

One rather hefty surgeon, ruefully surveying the divot he had scooped up from the Luffness fairway, was told by his caddy to 'tak' it hame and practise on it'.

Another, who spent most of his time retrieving his ball from the rough, heard his manservant mutter: 'It's a ferret he's needin', no' a caddy.'

But one golfer, finding his ball stuck in a rut on the 15th, ignored his caddy's sage advice: 'Pee on it and ca' it casual water.'

Who knows what dreadful scenes from this annual event have been forgotten. One recorder actually admitted, after a sojourn at the 19th hole: 'The spirit is strong but the memory is weak.'

THE drama of the golf Open doesn't compare with events at the seventh tee at Kinghorn. The occasion was the Jinglin' Geordie pub match, played by regulars from that serious Edinburgh hostelry.

Preparing to drive off was Jimmy Burnett, Edinburgh's housing committee chairman, a large man and a fabled clouter of the ball. And as luck would have it, this tee lies in a dip; so a significant 'gallery' was gathered above to watch what transpired.

Burnett's drive was as powerful as ever, carrying for a good 150 yards. But unfortunately it was not outstandingly accurate; in fact, it bounced off the tee marker and ended up 150 yards behind him.

Burnett then fluffed his second shot. So he was in the unique position of being two strokes down but still 30 yards short of the tee.

We will draw a veil over his thoughts. But a colleague said the position was an excellent analogy for the financial situation of local authorities everywhere.

DOUBLE entendre in One. From the American amateur champion Phil

Mickleson, being interviewed on television about weather conditions for the Open at Royal Birkdale: 'I think the wind is coming from my back side.'

THE British athletes and officials at the European Championships in Yugoslavia were startled to find that packets of condoms had been thoughtfully left in their hotel rooms. Even in the room of Miss Marea Hartman, 70, the chairwoman of the athletics board. 'I didn't know what they were,' she laughingly admitted.

At first, the athletes thought all this was the work of a practical joker; but it turned out to be a 'well-meaning' gesture by the organisers.

THE advance of black athletes in international track events was illustrated during a Grand Prix meeting at Meadowbank, Edinburgh. In the men's 400 metres, only one runner was white, and his name was Roger Black.

AGRI-JOURNALISTS at the Ingliston Winter Fair in Edinburgh were somewhat bemused when the organisers, keen to display a celebrity, produced the Scots athlete Yvonne Murray. She had just presented a champion dairy cow with its sash: but apart from that, what was her connection with the great world of farming?

At her press conference, however, Ms Murray showed she had pretty strong views on food. 'My own diet has been specially worked out,' said the runner. 'I eat 70 per cent pasta and carbohydrates. I am a firm believer in everything in moderation. When I'm abroad I can't believe that people eat meat every day . . . ' Wonderful stuff to hear in that hotbed of the beef industry. Notebooks ran hot.

WHEN the Scottish Commonwealth Games team left for Auckland, one member of the party took two cycling shoes — for the right foot only. The reason:

Arthur Campbell from Glasgow, a team official, had left earlier with the advance party. But in the rush, he had packed two left-footed shoes. The result was an urgent appeal to bring across their other halves.

There were no photographs available of Arthur attempting to cycle with one foot.

NO more congratulations, if you don't mind, for the 'fastest woman over 35' in the Inverness 10K People's Race. It just happens that the winner was a 'he' — John Watt, senior social development officer with the former Highlands & Islands Development Board.

The problem was that John and his wife Hilary both took part in the Inverness event; and when their race numbers came through the post, they pinned the wrong ones on their running gear.

When John came in at 38 minutes 51 seconds, the computer thought that he was his wife (although Hilary was a little further down the race field, taking about 52 minutes to finish the course).

So just stop phoning up to congratulate her on her success. It got rather embarrassing. Thanks.

THERE'S been a bit of controversy aired in *Scotland's Runner*, the joggers' bible, about the advisability of athletics clubs re-naming themselves to please sponsors. A rather puzzling example is that of the 'NOT Minolta Black Isle AAC'; editor Alan Campbell said he'd discovered 'NOT' stands for Northern Office Technology (Highlands) Ltd.

But in another twist, that company went into receivership, 'about six months after sponsoring Black Isle and getting a very public tie-up with an ambitious and successful club'. (Presumably, they are now the 'Not Necessarily NOT Minolta Black Isle AAC'.) Campbell urged clubs to think hard before changing their names.

A CRICKET match held at Twyford in Bristol, raised £44 for charity — but it cost the local cricket club £45 to replace a pavilion window which was smashed when an over-enthusiastic batsmen hit a six.

IT'S the quarter-finals of the men's singles and there's a pleasant smirr of rain. At Wimbledon, the covers would be over the courts and the brollies would be over the strawberries. But here, in Oban the tennis is hardier and nobody gives a toss.

In fact, the rules for the 20th West Highland Tennis Championships state, uncompromisingly: 'Weather — In the event of rain, players should report to the referee at the scheduled time for their matches.'

An official says: 'In West Highland tennis, it's the players who decide when the rain gets too much for them.' The drizzle is getting heavier. 'This is nothing. If they weren't prepared to play on, we'd never get finished.'

There are other ways, too, in which the Oban brand of tennis differs from Wimbledon. The referee is a teacher so can't be at the courts in school hours. Her deputy is supervising five matches simultaneously from the clubhouse windows.

There is a bit of confusion to the first day's play. Several competitors had to scratch when their cars wouldn't start, always a sign of a damp autumn. Also, some players have to slip off between matches to put in an appearance at work, or collect children from school. Keeping the schedule going is a bit of a jigsaw puzzle.

As a topspin drive skims the net, shaking off spray like a Catherine-wheel, more spectators turn up in anoraks. But by teatime, the tail-end of the Atlantic hurricane delivers serious rain and play has to stop.

TROON SAILING CLUB (no relation) was sinking slowly. Once it had around 200 members, but this fell to just 25. This was blamed on the amount of raw sewage on the beach and in the water as the area waited for a long overdue treatment plant.

The club commodore, Peter Connelly, described the situation as dangerous for yachtsmen who were unlucky enough to fall into the briny. 'The only advice I can give is — keep your mouth shut.'

AT the new £8.5 million Aonach Mor ski centre, next to Ben Nevis, a Gondola Cable Car System takes sportspeople and tourists 2,500 feet up to the Snow Goose Restaurant and Shop. There the management are lying in wait with a full range of goods and souvenirs that should keep the tills ding-donging merrily on high.

Some trinkets, we hear, will not be on show. There are the pencils which were supposed to bear the words 'Nevis Range' with a picture of a gondola car. Unfortunately, they arrived with an illustration of a Venetian gondola.

Equally puzzling were the T-shirts, which were supposed to carry the legend 'Ski the Goose' over a suitable picture. The picture turned out to be Donald Duck. Back to the drawing board.

OFFICIALDOM

L'euro-condom n'est pas arrivé, at least not yet. But it seems that harmonisation of this most topical gentlemen's perquisite is under way.

We understand that 1 July 1994 is the date by which all European Community partners (to employ a delicate double entendre) should be equipped in a manner which is fully approved by Brussels. But agreement over this one did not arrive easily.

It seems that the Italians attempted to halt efforts towards condom unification by proposing a ban on domestic sales of those which had a diameter greater than 53 mm, or 2.06 inches. The explanation for this piece of *unilateral dimensionism* is not given. Nevertheless, researches indicate that the average width of condoms sold in the United States is 2.02 inches.

Brussels bureaucrats responded to the Italians by saying that their restrictions amounted to a barrier to pan-European trade. Safety was also a concern, since condoms which were too small could split and expose partners to disease. (Or to pregnancy, although some people seem to overlook this point.)

In an exchange of memoranda, which we would dearly like the chance to fillet for satirical possibilities, the Italians backed down. Now EC standards will govern the quality and durability of condoms, but male Europeans themselves can make a choice of size.

Robin Gorna, a consultant to the director of social affairs in Luxembourg, pointed out, however: 'We're certainly not saying that European men should have the same size of apparatus by 1 July 1994.'

SUPPORTERS of three Edinburgh football clubs — Hearts, Hibs and Meadowbank — had to travel to Fife on the same night for Skol Cup ties. That just happened to be the night for a traffic census at the Forth Road Bridge. So if future statistics show that most Edinburgh football supporters live in Fife, you'll know why.

THE Deeside farmer granted planning permission to be buried along with his wife (eventually) on his own land was not alone in his search for a low-cost funeral. He wants the grave to be dug by his own mechanical digger, and to be laid in a home-made coffin of plywood. Estimate: £28 each.

Since then, *Which?* magazine turned its spotlight on funeral costs. It listed certain pre-payment packages, ranging from 'The Standard' at £640 to, intriguingly, 'The Lichfield' at £1,750.

But the magazine discovered Jane Spottiswoode, who organised her husband Nigel's cremation according to their shared belief that traditional funeral costs would be better spent on a party.

After many refusals, she managed to buy a chipboard veneer coffin from a wholesaler for £40. The departed was taken to the crematorium in a friend's estate car. She estimated that the DIY proceedings cost £500 less than the average funeral. Then, a couple of months afterwards, came the memorial party.

But here's the icing on the cake: since then Jane Spottiswoode has had a book published on the project, *Undertaken with Love*. If it does well, and the royalties flow in, she will even have upstaged the Deeside farmer.

THERE was an odd Catch 22 in the list of courses and seminars run by the Scottish Office Training Unit. The one-day class on 'assertiveness' is apparently available 'on demand'.

YOU can commission a pompous report on just about anything. So Edinburgh's Napier Polytechnic decided to have one on working standards in their lecture rooms.

'The first item on the agenda is the "blackboard environment", initially concentrating on the blackboard duster,' said the working party's report solemnly.

'The idea is that the blackboard duster should be placed in one of the compartments of the box at the side of the blackboard. If placed there immediately after use, this improves the cleanliness of the blackboard environment considerably.'

Unfortunately, the working party seemed to have very little faith in such a complicated procedure catching on quickly in the college.

'It will take this idea some time to percolate through all members of staff,' said the report, with an almost palpable sigh. Anyone who identified 'particular areas of non-compliance' (i.e. rebellious Napier Polytechnic lecturers who tossed the blackboard duster any old where) were invited to report this to the working party Chairman.

At first, we suspected that the whole report was a particularly subtle piece of satire on college life. But apparently, there's no such thing as blackboard humour.

IT was clearly with some relief that the Lay Observer, David Morrell, had his title changed to Legal Complaints Ombudsman. As he told reporters: 'When I first came across the title I thought it had something to do with the Egg Marketing Board.'

CANON KENYON WRIGHT said a mouthful when he told the Scottish Constitutional Convention's inaugural meeting in Edinburgh: 'From the great cities to the remotest Highland communities, the representatives of the people are here.' Behind this undeniable fact a well-laid plan lay hidden — a plan that concerns the thorny problem of travel costs.

That other convention, the Convention of Scottish Local Authorities (COSLA) — so often the target of St

Andrew's House suspicion because of its Labour domination — had done some quiet homework in advance. It discovered that because attendance at the Constitutional Convention would be considered a 'political' activity by the Scottish Office, those travelling to Edinburgh would not be able to claim a refund of travel expenses, or claim an attendance allowance.

Obviously, this would be a considerable deterrent to councillors from distant communities, such as the Shetland Islands. The trip would leave them £200 out of pocket.

But COSLA was already thinking along these lines. It reorganised its executive committee meetings so that they took place immediately before meetings of the Constitutional Convention — twice in Edinburgh, twice in Inverness, and once in Glasgow.

And, of course, all of those involved were entitled to claim attendance allowance and travel expenses to COSLA meetings. If these representatives, 'from the great cities to the remotest Highland communities', wanted to hang around and attend the Constitutional Convention as well, who could blame them? Rather neat, no?

NOT long after moving into a house under the Forth Bridge, a punter discovered an annoying phenomenon. Every time it rained, his house and his car parked outside were spattered with what appeared to be red paint, washed off the structure. This called for a letter to BR.

He didn't mind so much about the house (he wrote) as the paint wouldn't do it any harm. But the car was different, as its paint-work was being damaged. He suggested BR could build him a car-port, and added this postscript: 'If you could arrange to have the bridge moved eight feet to the left, it would be much appreciated.'

The reply from British Rail said that the red marks on the car were caused by dust from brake-pads, a well-known problem for houses underneath the bridge. However, the bridge was there before the houses and BR could not accept responsibility.

But the area civil engineer had given some thought to the compromise suggestion. 'A rough estimate for moving the bridge eight feet is £100 million. Perhaps you'd let me know if you're willing to pay half?' The correspondence ended there . . .

DELEGATES to a meeting of the Nuclear-Free Zones Scotland steering committee, hosted by Midlothian District at Dalkeith, talked peace studies and campaigned to have their backyards free of nuclear military menace. If they required a parking space, they were asked to contact a council official: a Mr Atack.

THERE was the Case of the Social Worker's Teeth. There was also the Case of the Home Help's Hair-do. The best brains in Lothian Regional Council wrestled with these matters for months.

Case 1: A regional social worker, in the course of his professional duties, was playing football with a bunch of kids. After a dramatic clearance from the goalmouth, the ball lodged in a tree. The social worker climbed up to retrieve it.

Sad to say, he fell from the tree and damaged his teeth. As his teeth were broken in the course of his employment, he asked the Social Work Department to pay for his dental treatment . . . but no luck.

Case 2: A regional home help was celebrating her wedding anniversary. First, she went to the hairdresser's and had an expensive perm. Then she had a wonderful night out with her family.

Shortly afterwards, she was sent in the course of her work to a house which turned out to be infested with fleas and lice. As a result of this, the home help had to be comprehensively deloused, a procedure which unravels the work of even the finest hairdresser. She asked her employers to reimburse her for the perm . . . but no luck.

These cases revealed a curious loophole in the region's compensation scheme. Under this scheme covering various injuries, employees can be recompensed for damage to false teeth or to a wig — but can't be compensated for damage to their own teeth or hair.

The issue was passed to and fro between the social work and personnel committees, and probably still is to this day.

RESIDENTS in the north of Edinburgh who complained about the horrible smells emanating from the Granton foreshore were interested to hear of the experience of a pollution control official.

While she was investigating the pong, ground water penetrated her protective clothing and damaged her jumper and trousers, and cleaning could not remove the stains or the smell.

She claimed £89.90 to replace the ruined items.

Also from the exciting, high-risk world of local authority service: an officer whose jacket and trousers became infested with fleas and had to have them sprayed by a pest-control officer; and a dog warden whose shirt sleeve and trousers were torn in two separate canine encounters.

Dedicated people, these.

DELEGATES turning up at a Scottish Recycling Forum in Glasgow were startled to find carefully laid plans for recycling something quite unexpected. To wit, them. Everyone's pack of conference papers included an organ donor card and a form to be completed.

Richard Morris, head of the Scottish Development Agency's energy and environmental technologies division, was perfectly frank about it. 'We don't only want to win your minds,' he told delegates. 'We want your bodies as well.

'This is the ultimate in recycling,' he added.

Delegates were urged to fill in the forms immediately. Otherwise, a great opportunity would have been lost if they suffered an untimely accident on their way home.

Other revelations at the conference were, perhaps, less surprising. For example, Ian Lang's announcement that the Scottish Office recycles 85 tons of paper a year . . .

A DROLL tale concerning the health of the planet was told during the Edinburgh Science Festival by none other than the chief scientist at the Department of Energy, Dr David Evans. It seems his staff wanted to practise what they are forever preaching by installing energy-efficient light bulbs in their London offices.

However, the bulbs are about three times larger than normal ones, and somewhat industrial-looking. The local authority had to be approached for planning permission, and this was refused. The council argued that the bulbs would upset the aesthetic beauty of the surroundings for the department's nearest neighbours.

What neighbours? The Royal Family, as it turns out — for the Department of Energy is overlooked by Buckingham Palace. Eventually, the department wore down the opposition — presumably ridiculing the idea that Her Majesty is prone to peering through her net curtains into other people's rooms. So, after considerable delay, the bulbs were installed and the planet was one notch safer.

IT'S always sad when a well-planned jape doesn't come off. That's what happened at Aberdeen, where Shell Expro decided to mark the coming on stream of their Osprey oilfield with a touch of ceremony at headquarters. Operations director Ian Henderson was to unveil a bronze sculpture of an osprey, by wildlife sculptress Mo Farquharson.

Shortly before the ceremony, someone at the company decided to have a little rehearsal. The cover was whipped off — and hey presto, the bronze osprey had laid an egg. Some joker had apparently obtained the egg from the canteen and craftily inserted it in the appropriate spot.

GOOD news. We hear of 'a new architecture for representing parsing of natural language which conforms to psycho-linguistic, neurolinguistic and computational restraints, using a neural-like computational scheme entailing a massive number of appropriately connected computing units that communicate through weighted levels of excitation and inhibition.'

The full story is available in Garrison Cottrell's *A Connectionist Approach to Word Sense Disambiguation*, published by Pitman.

Whatever happened to shorthand?

WE have survived European Year of Road Safety, of Cancer, of TV and Cinema, of the Environment, of the Disabled, and a European Year of Tourism.

These great causes are dreamed up by a small wheel somewhere in the vast machine of the European Commission, diligently dividing up the future and allotting each twelve-month to something or other. 1992, for example, was European Year of Safety at Work . . . 1993 European Year of the Elderly . . . 1994 will be . . . but wait a minute — what about 1991?

Funny you should ask that. European Year of the Elderly was supposed to be 1991, but organisational problems meant it had to be postponed until 1993. In the confusion, the commission forgot to choose a substitute. So 1991 was unique: European Year of Nothing At All.

This situation caused some confusion in the corridors of power at the Berlaymont, in Brussels. Some wits suggested that the only solution was to cancel 1991 altogether and call it 1992.

Another faction proposed European Year of Amnesia.

WE loved the apology distributed by HMSO: 'The publication *School Effectiveness Research* which was sent to you has many printing faults which we will correct in due *corse* by sending a replacement issue.'

POSTMEN have an awesomely public working life. Every householder along a postman's delivery route is aware of his comings and goings and any change in the routine is instantly detected.

Thus it was that a resident in Edinburgh's Portobello district was quick to notice that the morning's first delivery to his letterbox was being made an hour later than previously. He tackled the postman on this one and got what seemed like an amazing explanation.

'New instructions,' said the postie. 'I'm not allowed to keep crossing the road from side to side any more. I do the other side first and go into some other streets before I come down your side.'

Was this some startling new departure, perhaps emanating from the European Commission in Brussels? Will British postmen no longer cross the road, thus *harmonising* with postmen in Schleswig Holstein? The Diary tackled the Post Office, to discover that — no — this was simply a new rule applied to that particular walk in Portobello, and was made for safety reasons because of heavy traffic.

'But the round will still be completed by 9.30 a.m.,' we were told, 'and one addressee's loss will be another's gain.'

HOWEVER, a Montrose addressee had to wait a little beyond 9.30 a.m. for a letter from Linlithgow. As the postmark shows, it had been on the way for 330 years:

THIS was surely one of the great surreal moments in the annals of the Ministry of Defence. There was this chap on the phone, asking if they could lend him any old atom bombs, and he had a Belfast accent. All very innocent, as it happens, for the caller was Brian Gamble, chief executive of the Edinburgh International Science Festival. He thought an exhibition of old, unused A-bomb casings would have drawn a crowd: everyone has heard of them, but very few have had the opportunity to stroke or pat one.

'The MoD were the obvious people to ask,' said Gamble. But when he rang them up in Whitehall, the result was a controlled explosion of disbelief.

'They mentioned the fact that I sounded Irish. I agreed. So then they wanted to know what I was doing in Edinburgh. I explained again. But they didn't seem able to take the request seriously; they thought it was a send-up.'

Gamble tried again, asking a non-Irish-speaking member of staff to make the call this time. She drew a blank too, but Gamble is determined to try again. 'An A-bomb exhibition!' he enthused. 'People will queue for miles.'

THERE'S such a thing as the European Community Silly Ideas Industry — which thinks up rumours even more bizarre than some genuine Brussels directives. One surfaced in the seagoing community and was even reported by a yachting magazine.

Scottish fishermen are worried, it says, about a proposal concerning ships' medical supplies. In future, trawlers on trips lasting more than eight hours away from their home ports must carry 100 condoms, while those spending more than 24 hours at sea must stock 250 condoms.

This seemed like the most generous North Sea quota ever granted: but a European Community spokesman confirmed that it could be nothing more than a newly mongered rumour.

THINGS have come to a pretty pass when even local authority officials complain about gobbledegook in government communications. A housing manager was called in by a neighbour to help translate a note from the Inland Revenue, which ran:

The bank interest figure used is the 1987–88 figure which is assessable for 1988–89, the basis of assessment being first year current year basis, second year current year basis, third year current year basis or previous year basis to the advantage of the taxpayer, thereon previous year basis until the last two years when the last year is current year basis and the penultimate year is current year basis, or previous year basis to the advantage of the Inland Revenue.

At least the last seven words are clear enough.

COLLECTING the poll tax may be difficult, but it can also be difficult to prove you *have* paid the tax — as one Lothian resident discovered. An exchange of letters culminated in this mud-clear directive:

'If, after the imposition of a civil penalty under subsection (10) or (11) above but before the making of any appeal under subsection (12) below against that imposition, the Registration Officer, in the light of information which he did not consider when imposing the penalty (a) is no longer satisfied as to the matter as to which he was satisfied under paragraph (a) or (b) of subsection (10) above or paragraph (c) of subsection (11) above before imposing the penalty; or (b) is satisfied that the responsible person upon whom the penalty was imposed did have a reasonable excuse, he may revoke the imposition of the penalty; and on such revocation any money paid to the regional or islands council by the responsible person by way of that penalty shall be repaid by them to him.' In other words, the cheque might be in the post; or it might not.

IS there such a thing as a poll tax investigator with a sense of humour? This name appeared on a flat door in Marchmont, Edinburgh:

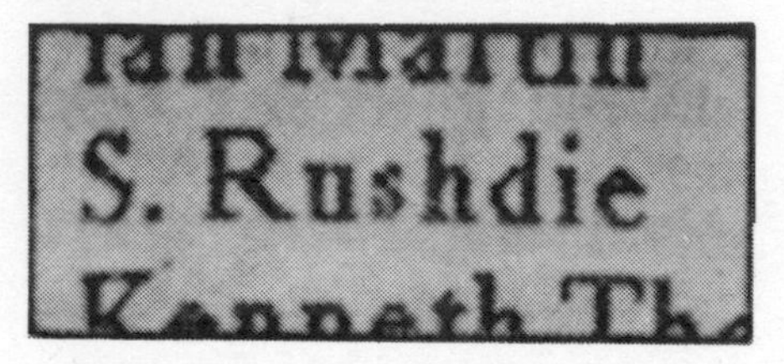

DO you always remember to put your clocks forward for British Summer Time? It didn't help a colleague who had to meet passengers on a British Midland flight from Malaga to Glasgow, due on Sunday.

He'd been given an arrival time of 5.25 a.m., but checked the night before. British Midland told him it would be in 'at 4.25 if you have not changed your watch, and 5.25 if you have'. So after an early rise on Sunday, he phoned again to see if the flight was on time, to be told that the flight was on schedule and would reach Glasgow at '4.25 a.m. local time'.

Question: 'Surely you mean 5.25 a.m. BST?'

Answer: 'Ah but, the clocks were put forward an hour in Spain at the same time as they were in Britain. Someone must have forgotten.'

When our man got to Glasgow Airport, he found the flight had already arrived — at 5.05 a.m.

The people he was meeting were also confused; the departure times at Malaga had been changed although nobody had altered the clocks. So they knew *where* they were, but they weren't sure *when*.

SOMEONE with a sense of humour and a taste for musical quotation must have designed one of Edinburgh's bin lorries. As they prepare to reverse and their crews, with many a song and a quip, collect the binbags of the day, a warning device sounds.

But instead of the usual beep-beep sound, one lorry played a tune recognisable as part of a phrase in Mendelssohn's overture to *A Midsummer Night's Dream*. Appropriately, this theme represents the entry of Billy Bottom and the 'rude mechanicals'. It is made up of two sets of triplets, one rising and one falling, as follows — diddle-dum, diddle-dum.

'This is new on me', said Edinburgh's director of cleansing. 'Are you sure? When we order new vehicles, we always stipulate that a continuous audible warning should sound when reverse gear is selected.

'This is made up of two notes — beep-boop-beep-boop — although we do have one lorry with a voice-tape which says "Stand clear . . . Stand clear". These devices are fitted by the manufacturers, and we have never ordered Mendelssohn. I would be really annoyed if anyone has tampered with an essential safety device.

'We have had occasional complaints from residents who find the sound irritating, especially in the early morning. But the whole purpose of the device is to give a warning.'

Certainly, it's a major advance on Hoffnung's celebrated works for orchestra and vacuum cleaners.

IF you heard of a sudden surge in the number of single-parent families in Lothian Region, you can blame SCAMP. This, of course, is a computer system — the Schools Computer Administration and Management Programme.

It took over from the well-known and completely reliable *pieces of paper* system of document storage, in which all information on primary school pupils is kept on file. But it did have a few wee drawbacks.

One Edinburgh head-teacher wrote to parents: 'I would like to apologise for the SCAMP .5 format, which does not allow for us to put in both parents' names in the box A2. As a result, we have had to enter the guardian's details at A2 and the other parent's details in the "Comments" section. Needless to say, all head-teachers have registered strong complaints, but to no avail.'

So with SCAMP relegating every second parent to a mere footnote, the future of the nuclear family does seem to be a trifle bleak.

SOME lethargic interest was inspired in the town of Peebles by the news that 'the showpiece Eastgate public toilets' were nominated for the 1991 Initial Loo of the Year Award. On such honours is civic pride founded.

However, the local *Peeblesshire News* told us that the Eastgate toilets were open 'for 70 hours in summer and 28 in winter'.

If true, this meant that taken over the whole year, these toilets were offering welcome relief for an average of less than two hours a week, during which time they were used by an average of 1,600 people.

It doesn't take a statistician to imagine that opening time at these particular public conveniences must be one of the great sights of the Borders burgh.

OUR imagination was also caught by the fascinating vital statistics of a hotel offered for sale in the old shire of Kinross. The hotel, we were told, includes 'two 40-seater restaurants, dining-room (140) and bathroom (250)', surely one of the most sociable loos you could hope to happen upon.

TWO neologisms – or new euphemisms to be more precise – arrived from the United States:

Gravitationally challenged: another way of calling somebody 'fat'.

Transparent wall engineer: window cleaner.

And for collectors of acronyms, we have:

Frumpies: formerly-radical upwardly mobile politicians.

LOTHIAN party chiefs found a crafty way round an embarrassing impasse at the Lothian and Borders Police Board. It began with the acting chairman,

Labour councillor Adam Montgomery, deciding that two of the three Tory members should be removed because, quite naturally, they were opposing Labour policies.

The Labour group leaders were mortified by this decision. It didn't have official backing and they put it down to the acting chairman's inexperience. So this is how it disappeared under the carpet:

Montgomery had to ask the board's clerk, R. L. Cowan, to put a motion for the removal of the two Tory members before the Lothian Regional Council. In order to do this, R. L. Cowan had to write to the regional secretary — R. L. Cowan.

The Labour and Tory groups got together and agreed that R. L. Cowan should send the letter to himself by second-class post. Thus it would arrive too late for the item to be included on the agenda for the regional council's next meeting. Because of holidays, the following meeting was six weeks away — by which time everyone would have forgotten about the problem. Simple, no?

WE have all heard about the wine lakes, butter mountains etc which supposedly stud the European landscape. But something even more alarming is on the horizon: a manure mountain.

The *European Parliament News* reported that Belgian Socialist member Marc Galle had, as it were, scented the growing danger and put a question to the Commission. He said manure surpluses had arisen from intensive stock-raising and that this was partly responsible for the fact that many rivers in the Community were 'biologically dead'.

In his reply, Commissioner Ray MacSharry said a temporary solution may lie in 'manure banks' — an interesting phrase, suggesting deposits and standing ordures. But, he sniffed, a permanent solution may be more difficult to find.

IN an ambitious bid for the annual Gobbledegook Award, Lothian's personnel department changed the rules on car mileage to read:

'8.1(d) that Heads of Department consider, in particular, the redesignation of casual users to essential users or consider the use of pool vehicles in situations where casual users are, on a consistent basis, claiming an average mileage over 3000 miles per annum, although such consideration shall not preclude redesignation of casual users to essential users under any aspect of the definition of essential user outlined in paragraph 6.5 above;

'8.1(f) that Heads of Department review the designation of essential user posts whenever such posts become vacant and the previous post holder consistently submitted average mileage claims below 3000 miles per annum, although any such review should not lead to a change in designation where the duties/requirements of the post are such that they comply with any other aspect of the definition of essential user outlined in paragraph 6.5 above.'

The bit we like best read: 'The above suggested changes are intended to clarify the meaning of the recommendations . . . '

GOOD news and bad news for a Lothian poll tax refusenik. He found a letter on his doormat to warn that his wages were to be arrested. But it came the day after he had lost his job.

A POLLTAX registration form, sent to an address in Crieff, was returned to the registration office with a rather abrupt reply. The envelope was marked 'Gone Away. Try the Crematorium.'

IN Glasgow parlance, *Aw horo, whit an awfy shame*. But this is what happened in the city which had just spent an entire year and a fortune on encouraging the creative arts.

The scene was Glasgow's Botanic Gardens, under a six-inch blanket of pristine snow. A group of children and their nannies were doing what children have always done when confronted with an abundance of this seasonal material: building a snowman.

Enter a park-keeper — a most apologetic gent, as it turned out. He was sorry, but he had his instructions from above. Nae snowmen. Following his orders, he then kicked the snowman down and redistributed the snow until no sign of the kids' creation remained. Exeunt some very confused children indeed, along with some very indignant nannies.

A spokesman for Culture City told the Diary that trampling snow into the turf can ruin a lawn. 'The kids just happened to choose the only two acres of grass in our 70 parks where walking is forbidden. This lawn is in front of the Kibble Palace and the glasshouses; we like to keep it looking nice.'

Clearly, the snow melted before any hearts did on this one.

THE British Army was far from *at ease* as it faced yet another round of rumours about regiments disappearing or amalgamating in the defence cuts. It seems like only yesterday — although it was two decades ago — that purse-string-tightening produced what came to be known as the 'vulgar fraction' regiments, the 17th/21st Lancers for example.

This led to a rather nice spoof in *Soldier* magazine when Britain was going about introducing decimal currency. The magazine claimed it had uncovered secret MoD plans to decimalise the Army as well. Thus:

- 17th/21st Lancers would become 0.961 Lancers.
- 16th/5th The Queen's Royal Lancers would become 3.2 The Queen's Royal Lancers.
- The Royal Regiment of Wales (24th/41st Foot) would become The Royal Regiment of Wales (0.585 Foot), but would probably have to be converted into centimetres.

Who knows what's ahead for the soldiery next. In the longer term, they might have to be expressed in ECU.

SUPERSTITION is alive and well in the Royal Navy. Or perhaps we should call it good sense. Anyway, a new Type 23 frigate being fitted out at Yarrow's on the Clyde — HMS *Lancaster* — had its pennant number changed with the approval of the MoD. It was to have been F 232: but this is also the designation of the form which has to be filled in to report a grounding or a collision. The ship thus became F 229, to the relief of all who will sail in her.

EDINBURGH'S bureaucrats introduced a new citizens' charter on 'customer care', which seemed to involve district council staff answering their telephones promptly, sounding friendly and wearing name-tabs in the front office. Nothing wrong with that.

But there was a swift riposte from Midlothian District Council headquarters in Dalkeith. The Midlothian punter, we learned, had been getting this sort of deal since staff were sent on a Hotel and Catering Training Board course on being nice.

We rather liked the 'before' and 'after' comparisons on telephone answering techniques:

'Hello. Mr who? Who is it? What? I can't hear you. Speak up!' ('Hello, I'm sorry the line's not very clear. I can't hear you. Could you speak a little louder?')

'Hold on, your request was here, but it seems to have vanished . . . no, someone must have taken it. Just a minute. I'll get something to write that down.' ('I don't have your file here at the moment, could I take a note of the details and call you back.')

Then there's the 'out to lunch' clanger: 'He's at lunch. No, I don't know when he'll be back. Sorry, I don't know anything about that. There's absolutely nothing I can do.' This magically becomes: 'I'm sorry, he's not available . . . '

And the really girny one that goes: 'That's typical. No one tells you anything in this place,' is massaged into 'I'm very sorry, it seems there's been a misunderstanding.' You have to admit that the bad examples are more fun.

NO PERSONS IN TRAFFIC WARDENS UNIFORM WILL BE SERVED IN THIS SHOP

M A WILSON

WAS this it at last — the long-awaited popular uprising against traffic wardens? This notice appeared in a butcher's shop in Edinburgh's Royal Mile. We gather it followed a discussion when a van stopped outside the shop to unload sides of beef.

As anyone who has attempted to lift half a bullock will testify, it is not the sort of thing you take on a half-mile hike. Yet up clumped the jackboots and out came the sticky tape. Let *them* walk for their mince in future, the butcher decreed.

THE Open University is a hotbed of seriousness. Staff and students are concerned with life-enhancing knowledge, grey-matter stimulation, better prospects etc, through a bewildering range of esoteric lectures. But clearly, there is a maverick or two among them: for an 'Alternative Prospectus' appeared on the noticeboard at an OU study centre. Here's a selection from the 30-odd courses on offer:

- Self Improvement — Creative Suffering; Overcoming Self-Doubt through Pretence and Ostentation; Feigning Knowledge (A Career Advancement Strategy); Guilt Without Sex; Carrying a Piece of Paper While Walking Briskly.

- Business & Career — Packaging and Selling Your Child; An Underachiever's Guide to Very Small Business Opportunities; Supply Teaching in the Falklands; Credit Purchasing with your Kidney Donor Card.
- Arts & Crafts — Bonsai Your Pet; Self-Actualisation Through Macramé; Drawing Genitalia in Soft Pastel Shades (Summer-term only).
- Home Economics — Cultivating Viruses in the Household Refrigerator; Basic Kitchen Taxidermy; Khmer Rouge Cookery for Beginners.
- Fitness & Health — Snap Out of It/ Pull Yourself Together (Full Credit Course); Tap Dance Your Way to Social Ridicule; Eating with Plastic Spoons.

THEN there was an outbreak of the same at the BBC.

An extensive range of 'Staff Assertiveness Courses' attracted puzzled interest at Broadcasting House in Glasgow.

Some of the suggestions are well-worth pondering:

- Creative Suffering;
- Dealing with Post-Realisation Depression;
- Keeping Facts out of Production Meetings;
- Tattooing your Colleagues as an Income Supplement;
- Guilt Without Sex;
- 1001 Other Uses for a Sony Walkman;
- Bonsai Your Producer;
- Basic Office Taxidermy.

WE were fascinated to learn that an updated Vatican Latin Dictionary was being published, with the first volume, A-L, coming out just before Christmas, in good time for students' stockings. You might ask why — with the Tridentine Mass outlawed — the Vatican felt such an exercise essential.

The answer is that while national languages are now used by priests administering to their flocks, Latin is still the language of official Vatican documents.

Thus, the following terms were being added to the lexicon:

- Slot-machine: *sphaeriludium electricum nomismate actum.*
- Discothèque: *orbium phonographicorum theca.*
- Dishwasher: *escariorum lavator.*
- Cover-girl: *exterioris pagine puella.*

Clearly, the cardinals were preparing themselves to deal with some unusually interesting subjects.

AS ever, the people of Biggar were being kept one step ahead of the rest of us by the flow of useful information printed in their community council news sheet.

When February's issue plopped through the letterboxes, the 'Diary of Events' contained this handy piece of advice: 'Sunday 25 — British Summertime begins. Advance clocks one hour.'

Throughout the rest of Britain, of course, BST was to begin on 25 March.

Biggar residents faced the prospect of an extra hour's late drinking in the pubs (which would open an hour later in the morning) and bus travellers to Lanark would arrive there a quarter of an hour before they left home.

MAYBE the Scottish Egg Producer Retailers Association was reassuring members by pointing out that the food poisoning problem was worldwide.

One issue of the association's market report passed on the sad tale of a very posh Japanese wedding where the unfortunate guests were provided with sushi.

'This consists of raw meats very thinly cut, such as fish and even whalemeat,' said the report. 'A lot of the guests went down with food poisoning and 13 died.

'At a funeral wake held later for the 13, again sushi was provided . . . and eight of the mourners died.'

So, in effect, there.

A 'Quality Assurance Conference ' at Edinburgh City Chambers dealt esoterically with the quality of life or otherwise on peripheral housing estates.

Words like *disempowerment* abounded: also sentences like: *Implicit also is a system of beliefs or values by reference to which decisions are made with regard to both purposes and means.*

But for serious double-take, we recommend this thought from the Community Empowerment Workshop: 'It is important to recognise that people do not necessarily want to act out the roles following from every decision they are party to. If it is my decision to wear neatly pressed clothes, doing my own ironing may well detract from rather than serve that purpose.'

Now is that completely clear?

THE public inquiry at Cockburnspath under the 1949 Coast Protection Act made history in two ways, its participants felt. It was the first public inquiry ever held under the Act, and it was probably the coldest public inquiry *since records began.*

The inquiry opened in the local church hall on one of the bitterest mornings for a while, and participants arrived to find the heating system not operating. They sat in scarves and overcoats, listening to the latest on coastal erosion at Cove Harbour. The hall was also used for Sunday school, and to complete everyone's misery, a verse was seen pinned to the wall:

January brings the snow,
Makes our feet and fingers glow . . .

NATURALLY, scientists at the applied ecology research group at the Central London Polytechnic were dismayed when they read in the *Times Higher Education Supplement* that they were in the process of studying the life cycle of the little people who are generally depicted sitting on toadstools.

Two members of staff wrote in to protest most vehemently.

'We are certainly not working on elves,' they declared, 'nor on gnomes, fairies, witches or any such phantasmagoria. We are working on studies of elvers, which, as everyone knows, are the young migrant stages of eels (*Anguilla anguilla L.*).'

So endeth another interesting rumour.

STUDENTS at Glasgow Polytechnic joined in the debate over a new name for the place as it went for university status. The favourite was 'Kelvin University', with its degrees to be known as 'Kelvins'. As every budding physicist knows, 'Kelvin' means absolute zero degrees on a thermometer.

ALL sorts of interesting problems were cast up by the new arrangements under which family doctors could become 'fund-holding practices' and place 'contracts' for specialist services.

The British Medical Association's East Anglian regional consultants' committee was told of a small complication that arose when a practice in Norwich chose to assign its pathology requirements to a hospital in Great Yarmouth.

But Great Yarmouth is a 20-mile drive from Norwich. When the time came to send what is apparently known as 'a hot stool sample' to the pathologists, the journey proved too much for it; it was unusable.

So it was suggested to the poor patient that she should drive the 20 miles herself and deposit another sample in person. Apparently, she wasn't very impressed.

MEETINGS of the Scottish region committee of the Coalfields Community Campaign were cherished among shorthand note-takers for their down-home rhetoric. For example:

- 'These particular *thingummies* have to be highlighted and put to the front.'
- 'It should be a getting-together situation, a full-steam-ahead situation.'
- 'You are wearing two hats and speaking with a forked tongue.'

There could be a new Chambers dictionary in this, surely.

HERE'S a little-known fact that should go down well in the Home Counties:

If the 65 million tonnes of farmyard manure produced each year by Britain's livestock was piled along the M1 between Maidenhead, Berkshire, and London, it would reach a height of 200 feet.

This interesting statistic was provided to the Institute of Agricultural Engineers annual meeting at Bridge of Allan by Dr Brian Payne, from a research centre in Berkshire oddly enough. But it was apparently just a thought, not a suggestion.

WE heard a jolly tale about the quality of life in Edinburgh — something that was drawing undue attention to the place before, mysteriously, it was overtaken by Perth. It happened during the analysis of results from a survey, commissioned by Edinburgh District Council and conducted by a market research company.

When the first draft of responses was delivered to the district council, the pen-pushers at City Chambers noticed something odd. It seemed residents were concerned about a hitherto unsuspected trend — the loud and insistent use of ghetto-blasters in the douce capital.

There was a swift flurry of inquiries, and the misunderstanding was tracked down to a typing mistake. The residents were responding to a question on control of radioactivity — not radio activity.

THE civil service is well known for its love of 'proper channels', but this is ridiculous. During rebuilding work next to New St Andrew's House in Edinburgh, home of the Scottish Office, the following notice appeared on a doorway: 'Fire Exit: Authorised Persons Only'.

CITY HALL

THE gung-ho Conservative group on Edinburgh District Council supports the principle of putting services out to tender. It may even be fair to say that when such contracts are awarded 'in-house', the Tories look on the arrangements with a jaundiced eye.

But anyway: the Conservative group duly had their Christmas lunch in the City Chambers dining-room, cooked and served by the Catering Direct Services Organisation. There was one amusing moment when two of the Tories, Christine Richard and Lindsay Walls, had to abandon their food and dash off urgently to a meeting — of the dreaded direct service organisation committee.

But the *pièce de résistance* came at the end of the meal. The Tories were served with Christmas pudding and brandy sauce. But instead of sugar, the sauce appeared to have been laced with salt. 'It was revolting,' one councillor told us. 'We complained about it immediately.'

Oh well, innocent mistakes sometimes happen. Don't they?

THE coat which Glasgow's Lord Provost, Susan Baird, wore to welcome the Queen was much admired. In technical terms, the Diary gathers, it is a 'red Mansfield'. Thus, when somebody spotted a 'red Mansfield' in Edinburgh, confusion set in.

'Hello Lord Provost,' she began. 'Did you ever get that video of the ice show we sent you?'

But the Lord Provost looked completely mystified. And no wonder — for she was the Lord Provost of Edinburgh, Eleanor McLaughlin. Wearing exactly the same coat.

With two women heading Scotland's biggest cities for the first time in history, this sort of thing was probably on the cards.

THE former Lord Provost of Edinburgh, Eleanor McLaughlin, was invited to take part in the opening ceremonies of Dublin 1991 — European City of Culture. At least she though she had been invited. The letter came addressed as follows:

> The Rt. Hon. Cllr. Susan Baird,
> Lord Provost,
> City Chambers,
> High Street,
> EDINBURGH EHI 17J

Susan Baird is, of course, the Lord Provost of Glasgow, the 1990 Euroean City of Culture — a fact which is well known to the Lord Mayor of Dublin, Michael Donnelly, who signed the invitation.

So the Diary got in touch with Glasgow City Chambers — and sure enough, the invitation to Susan Baird referred to her as Eleanor McLaughlin.

This promised to lead to an entire weekend of confusion, as the two Lord Provosts grappled with misleading seating plans at the formal dinner, two lunches and supper — to say nothing of identifying themselves to the flunkey at the State Reception.

In the previous item the Diary reported that by pure coincidence, Eleanor McLaughlin and Susan Baird had chosen exactly the same model of red winter coat as they carried out their various civic duties. Well, this is the result.

Don't say we didn't warn them.

DEATH in East Lothian — where is thy sting? That area's district council had the following entry in the telephone directory: 'Cemeteries — see listing under Leisure, Recreation and Tourism'.

A FLURRY of constitutional apathy followed a motion, passed by Edinburgh Central Labour Party, to press for a sort of delayed-action abolition of the monarchy. Obviously, the party doesn't want to rush into these things too quickly: but touchingly, it would like to see Prince Charles have his shot at the throne first.

The motion, from the Dalry-Shandon Branch, said the monarchy should be abolished 'after the death or abdication of King Charles'. Apparently, this would give the royal family time to get used to the idea. But also, it turned out that Edinburgh Central socialists had a soft spot for the heir.

One constituency member told the Diary he was 'gobsmacked' when the motion appeared on the agenda. Those putting it forward were obviously torn between their opposition to 'an outdated institution' and the fact that — following his outspoken pronouncements on everything from modern architecture to global warming — they thought Charles 'wasn't such a terribly bad guy'.

Due consideration was also given to the assumption that by the time King Charles succeeded to the throne he would be well into his middle years. Therefore his turn was bound to be shorter than Queen Victoria's epic reign, for example.

The member said: 'Sometimes there is not much point in opposing motions like this. You just let them go through. I presume the royal family will not be rushing north to Edinburgh to receive their instructions.'

ALARMING news at Fife Region's financial planning sub-committee. An item on the agenda suggested support for a conference organised by Community Business Scotland, who were 'responsible for creating 3,000 jobs in areas of economic and social depravity'.

IT took an exiled Glaswegian to think this one up. A Glasgow-born reader, living in Edinburgh, was surprised by lack of local knowledge about the capital city's coat of arms and motto. The arms show an . . . err . . . and the motto runs . . . oh dear, we see what she means.

Every Glasgow child, on the other hand, is familiar with *that* city's arms, thanks to the well-worn ditty about the bell, the tree, the fish etc.

So she designed some new Edinburgh arms, shown here, drawn by professional illustrator Val MacAdam.

It brings together those legendary Edinburgh items, the fur coats and the cancelled drawers. The Latin motto is as near as Edinburgh University classics department can come to 'You'll have had your tea?'

The Lord Lyon will be along there at the toot to *ding her doon*, we have no doubt.

BUT that idea had an echo in the west. Every Glaswegian knows the jingle about that city's crest. But this new visual interpretation now appears in the best café-bars, worn on T-shirts:

the Bells... the Fish... & the Tree.

TALES about politicians' docile responses to chain letters sparked off a curious example, circulating among some female councillors in Edinburgh City Chambers. It ran:

'This letter was started by a woman like yourself, in the hope of bringing relief to other tired and discontented women. Unlike most chain letters, this one does not cost anything. Just send a copy of this letter to five of your friends who are equally tired and discontented. Then bundle up your husband or boyfriend, send him to the woman whose name appears at the top of the list, and add your name to the bottom of the list.

'When your name comes to the top you will receive 16,877 men, and one of them is bound to be a hell of a lot better than the one you already have.

'Do not break the chain. Have faith. One woman broke the chain and got her own b . . . d back. At this writing, a friend of mine had already received 184 men. They buried her yesterday, but . . . ' and here the letter descends into certain indelicacies. Deplorable.

IT was a trail of high adventure as members of Lothian social work committee carried out their duties on behalf of poll-taxpayers.

One group found itself inspecting an unused 200-year-old mansion called St Katherine's, at Howdenhall. The building was boarded up, but a side door was found to be open. As the councillors tip-toed through the spooky interior, they could hear distant barking, as if from the ghosts of forgotten family hounds.

The barking came nearer and nearer (and, of course, less and less ghostly) until the inspection party found itself confronted by three manifestly non-dead alsatians. The councillors had stumbled upon a training session for guard dogs.

As the committee scattered, the dogs went with unerring instinct for only one of them — Cllr Brian Fallon. It was only afterwards that his colleagues could work out why. In real life, Cllr Fallon is a postman. (But nevertheless, he was unscathed.)

More councillors were visiting a soup kitchen for down-and-outs in the Royal Mile. As they spoke to the supervisor, she was approached by a decrepit old gent requesting a cup of tea. She directed him to the canteen counter; but after collecting his cuppa, the gent insisted on rejoining the party at their table.

The supervisor was just about to send him off when the councillors intervened. 'It's all right,' they said. 'He's with us. He's on the social work committee too.'

'COUNCILLOR KNOCKS OUT GUIDE DOG — OFFICIAL'. Not a headline you come across too often, but what happened was this:

Des Loughney, a Lothian Regional councillor and secretary of Edinburgh Trades Council, was walking briskly along a city street. Swinging from his hand was the huge briefcase stuffed with papers which is reckoned to be his trademark.

Coming towards him was a blind woman with her guide dog. As they passed, the dog was distracted by a loud noise from the street traffic. It turned towards the sound and — clunk — caught the full force of the Loughney briefcase on the side of the head.

To the councillor's dismay, the dog collapsed and rolled over, out for the count. What could be worse for the image of a caring member of the Labour group?

As Loughney explained to the puzzled woman what had happened to her faithful companion, the dog struggled groggily to its feet, shook itself, and prepared to go about its duties again.

The councillor gave his phone number in case there were any problems; but this was evidently one tough dog, for he has heard nothing more.

The irony is that Des Loughney really is something of an animal lover. He once did something that few people would take on: he looked after a neighbour's pet python during the holidays.

Well, unfortunately, the python took refuge in the chimney, from where no amount of tail-tugging would coax it. Des had to call out the python retrieval specialists.

ON another occasion, the accident-prone councillor was innocently preparing to cross the road when a temporary sign fell on his head. It read 'Pedestrians Cross Here', and there can be little doubt that he was pretty cross at that.

A DIFFERENT kind of problem faced Edinburgh's former Lord Provost, Eleanor McLaughlin. Unlike royalty, she found it necessary to carry some cash from time to time. On her way to a function in her official car, she asked the driver to pull up at a cash dispenser. Out she popped chain of office dangling from her neck.

As she got back into the car, her chauffeur said helpfully: 'I could have done that for you, Lord Provost.'

Mrs McLaughlin: 'What? And let you know my cash-card number?'

MEMBERS of the newly amalgamated Caithness and Sutherland Local Health Council were told of an initiative to establish an alcohol counselling service in the area.

They agreed that anything to help problem drinkers was a good idea. But they were slightly bemused to learn that discussions would be held at a cheese and wine soirée in a Golspie hotel.

EDINBURGH councillor William Samuel took his three-year-old son, Peter, to the City Chambers so that the sprog could see where dad spent all those hard-working hours away from home.

The youngster took one look round the nicotine-veiled magnificence of the Smoking Room and inquired loudly: 'Is this the Jinglin' Geordie then?' — naming the pub with which Labour group members are not unacquainted.

TOASTS to the European ideal were no doubt drunk heartily when Edinburgh District Council gave a civic reception to delegates, architects etc from the French town of Auxerre.

However, the European ideal has not yet reached the point where councillors from Scotland and France can converse easily in one another's lingo. So an interpreter was brought in, and she took her role seriously, going to great pains to introduce strangers to one another.

Perhaps her greatest triumph was to lead a group of Edinburgh Tories across to a group of Edinburgh Labourites, and ask whether they would like to talk to each other. She even offered to interpret (which, no doubt, would have been necessary).

SURVIVAL is the name of the game when Edinburgh planning committee members go on site visits on a wet and windy day. For this reason, Tory member David Guest brought along a plastic carrier bag containing a pair of the traditional green wellies.

But when the time came to wade through some mud, he discovered to his consternation that the wellingtons were not a pair: one was a woman's size. Also, they were both for the same foot.

Labour colleagues on the council reported with delight that, naturally, they were both for the right.

ONE of the features of these *very important conferences* — which frequently take our elected representatives to seaside resorts — is the trade souk. Outside the conference hall, various suppliers, pressure groups etc set up their stalls and wait to hook influential people, such as Tom Ponton, the Tory Lothian Regional councillor for Murrayfield/Dean.

Ponton was taking a breather from the social work conference in Eastbourne by walking through the exhibition area when one persistent trader asked him for his card. He knew he was a busy man: he'd send him some samples.

These duly arrived: a parcel of incontinence bags. Much ribald laughter, of course. The councillor, who hadn't known exactly what to expect, surely passed them on to a good home.

IN the United States, the word 'bum' does not suffer from any scatological inference; it means 'tramp'. In fact, it is a suitable name for a dog, and the town mascot of San Diego, California, from 1886 to 1898 answered to that very monosyllable.

San Diego is one of Edinburgh's twin cities. So to mark this connection, a bronze statuette of the dog now rests on a plinth in Edinburgh City Chambers. But without this lengthy explanation, it's not surprising that the card marking the gift causes unseemly mirth among those who come across it for the first time. It reads:

Bum was presented to the Lord Provost by the President of the Gaslamp Quarter Foundation.

THE civic limousines of Scotland's two major cities have provided the citizenry with many an ironical laugh over the years. But Edinburgh's city Daimler achieved a new peak of civic embarrassment by breaking down outside a shop owned by the councillor who has been its severest critic.

It happened as the chauffeur was on his way to pick up the Lord Provost, Eleanor McLaughlin, to take her to the Edinburgh Gold Cup meeting at Musselburgh racecourse. He stopped outside a newsagent's in Causewayside to make some purchases — and when he returned to the Daimler with its cherished (if tarnished) number plate S-0, the so-and-so wouldn't start.

The chauffeur had to ask for helpers to push the Daimler to a safer parking spot. And that is how the newsagent, Conservative councillor Lindsay Walls, who has spoken out in debates more than once about Labour's limo-policy, found himself actually giving his *bête noire* a shove.

Because the council's transport department was closed for a local holiday, the Daimler had to be taken away in disgrace by a local garage on its low-loader, and the Lord Provost of Scotland's capital had to be driven to Musselburgh in a Ford Sierra.

Naturally, Councillor Walls could hardly conceal his satisfaction at this gift from the Gods of Publicity. 'We've had this car since 1983,' he said. 'A special fund was set up to replace the city Daimler every three years — but the Labour administration has spent the money on something else.'

Previous civic limousine amusement was provided by Edinburgh's 13-year-old Rolls Royce, sold in 1983 after being off the road for two years. Glasgow's 14-year-old Rolls, meanwhile, required a £41,000 overhaul — and when that city's Lord Provost visited Edinburgh in a Daimler in 1986, the car disgraced itself by catching fire. Unlike the cars in question, this saga could still run and run.

THERE'S sometimes an outbreak of poetry amongst the city fathers and mothers. One poet celebrated a fall suffered by Eleanor McLaughlin in the following terms:

Unfortunate Accident
In City Chambers

The Lord Provost of Edinburgh fell
Down the stairs on her bahookie;
Though she was sober
She couped right over —
And now she's wearing a stookie.

THE muse was also busy at a dinner in Peebles when the hosts were British Coal.

Before the assembled guests hit the trough, it was suggested (for reasons of courtesy, perhaps) that the grace might be said by Councillor Peter Boyes, of Lothian Regional Council.

Now Councillor Boyes just happened to be the Scottish chairman of the Coalfields Community Campaign, whose differences of opinion with British Coal are obvious.

Overcome with the unexpected source of his free meal, he came out with: 'For what we are about to receive, may the Lord be truly thankful.'

A reasonable standard of satire was then maintained in a competition for rhyming slogans promoting the fossil fuel which has all but disappeared from Scottish production.

A delegation from Edinburgh District Council won first prize in the competition with:

If ye're feelin' cauld the night,
Tak hame a bag o' anthracite.

For a close second we had the rather dubious couplet:

If perchance you should expire,
Burn yourself on a real coal fire.

But it was a local politician whose ward includes a significant proportion of council housing who won the star prize. He had to complete a promotional slogan on the delights of a real coal fire, and came up with:

I like a real fire because . . . you get rehoused immediately.

THERE was this poor Paisley buddy who couldn't get any sleep. There seemed to be a bird in her attic, chirping away through the night.

It was driving her mad. She got in touch with her councillor, Jim Mitchell of the SNP. As she spoke to him, he could clearly hear the maddening chirp down the phone.

He got in touch with Environmental Health. Yes, they said, there had been trouble with pigeons in that area. They had to chase a whole flock of them from a nearby house and block up the holes they'd made in the eaves. They'd go round to investigate this new mischief as soon as possible.

But they were busy, and another week passed with the poor buddy getting no sleep. The councillor prodded Environmental Health again. 'We're sending two of our best men,' they told him, 'right away.'

At the house, armed with all the latest in bird-catching equipment, the men started to stalk their quarry. But — no bird. And just as they were about to leave the chirping started again. It sounded like a bird's distress signal.

Up in the attic they found . . . a smoke detector alarm, designed to give out a chirruping signal when its battery is running low. It was supplied, in fact, by Renfrew District Council. Not knowing whether to laugh or cry, the exhausted tenant decided to have a good sleep instead.

MORE on environmental health matters. This is, of course, the department which deals with unwelcome wasps' nests on roofs and in gardens, and a very busy summer they'd been having.

Indeed, one citizen who phoned the department requesting the removal of a wasp clan from his garden, was told it would take three weeks. The chap they would have sent for the operation was off sick. He'd been stung by a wasp.

A spokesman confirmed the sad news and said the pest control officer had suffered a 'bad reaction' from the sting. But the good news is that the wasps were so disgusted by the delay that, after waiting for a few days, they all died voluntarily.

FAULDHOUSE is a small place, so everybody must know what everyone else is up to. Wrong. A young couple from the old mining village, touring in the north, called into a shop in Forres to find the proprietor engrossed in a book entitled *A History of Fauldhouse Victory Cricket Club*. It was written by their local West Lothian district councillor who happened to live next door to the wife's mother. They were so surprised to discover he was an author, and that his book on this undoubtedly absorbing subject was being read 200 miles away, that they clean forgot to buy a copy.

STRANGE event at Lothian Region. The chairman of the Lothian and Borders Fire Board, Cllr Bill Axon, was making a phone call when a colleague burst in. 'That's the fire alarm!' he shouted.

Axon apologised. 'I'm sorry, I can't listen to you at the moment,' he said. 'I'm in the middle of a call.' At the other end of the phone was — Peter Scott, the Firemaster.

THE Iraqi 'supergun' was clearly not forgotten by Edinburgh's planning committee. At first, councillors might not have been alarmed unduly by an application to erect a 'large diameter stainless steel external flue' in the New Town: then it was noticed that the request was signed 'S. Hussain'. Application refused.

Who said the planning committee wasn't patriotic?

IN one of those quirky little procedures that make local authority-watching so enjoyable, Edinburgh's director of administration had to prepare a report for the district council's policy and resources committee about his own salary.

He was owed a 'temporary higher duties allowance' for the two months when he was acting as the council's chief executive; and perhaps not surprisingly, he recommended that the dosh should be paid to his good self.

The report reassured councillors on the committee that the wee bonus of £468.50p could be contained, no bother, within his department's budget. Payment approved.

If only real life could be as simple.

THE coming of the 'superloo' to Aberdeen was attended by spectacular mishaps. Several of these high-tech, press-button conveniences were put in place by the Labour-led city council, anxious that the outlying housing schemes should not miss out on this automated experience.

They were supposed to be vandal-proof: but this must have been interpreted as a challenge. One of the devices, in Byron Square shopping centre, Northfield, was reported not to have worked for more than 24 hours at a stretch.

On one occasion, an anonymous user cunningly switched the labels identifying the control buttons. The next incumbent, an unfortunate woman, pressed the button marked 'toilet paper' — upon which the door immediately flew open.

An environmental health spokesman said: 'There have been teething troubles. The superloos are declared vandal-proof, but we seem to have a particularly ingenious type of vandal.'

FROM the North Tayside Conversative Association campaign newsletter:

> The SNP group of Councillors on Tayside Region must be the most incompatant group in the country.

THE Remembrance ceremony in Edinburgh is something which former Lord Provost Eleanor McLaughlin is, aptly enough, unlikely to forget. She was arriving at the Garden of Remembrance in Princes Street, where photographers and TV crews waited along with a considerable crowd, when she discovered she was wearing one black shoe and one blue.

However, Princes Street is renowned for having lots of shoe shops, and quick as a flash she was across the road, tried on a matching pair of black, and the startled shop assistant had made the quickest sale in her career.

The truth emerged later at the City Chambers, when an eagle-eyed colleague spotted a label with the tell-tale information: £19.99. 'New shoes, Eleanor?' he inquired.

'Aha,' she said, 'there's a wee story behind that . . . '

THERE was some impolite laughter in Edinburgh City Chambers over the planned 'Information Day'. The public were invited to a five-hour event during which the City Fathers and Mothers would explain their carefully-laid budget and policy plans for the coming financial year. For further information, the public were asked to contact two city officials — named Malarky and Alcock.

FOR the Forth Bridge Centenary celebrations, Lothian Region pressed into use its infamous sludge vessel, the *Gardyloo*. The boat set out upon the briny, bearing those and such as those, who could then watch the fireworks while sinking a snifter or two. A creative official named this malodorous junket *The Slurry with the Binge on Top*.

WHEN the Soviet coup against Gorbachev failed, Renfrew District Council was so moved that it appointed its SNP and Labour group leaders to pen a telegram of congratulations — thus becoming the only Scottish local authority to open such a dialogue.

The victors of the counter-coup were praised for their courage and determination, admired for their bravery and resolution, and congratulated for their momentous victory in the name of freedom.

And then — oh dear — the telegram was sent to the Russian ambassador in London, Leonid Zamyatin. You know, the one who was recalled to Moscow after declaring that the coup was lawful . . .

THERE'S such a thing as local authority patois. And in case somebody is compiling a phrase-book, here are a few useful entries:

- *Homologate* is a verb which you will only come across in a Scottish council's minutes. It means to ratify by a subsequent decision. But the Diary had it on good local authority that at a recent committee meeting of one West of Scotland district council, a member declared: 'This decision must go to the full council for to be humiliated.'
- From another council committee, there's word of an important new aphorism, issued in tones of dire warning: 'A leopard can't change horses in midstream.'
- From the smoke-room at Renfrew District Council we heard of a conversation concerning the availability of council housing in the desirable — to say nothing of middle-class — district of Kilbarchan. The subject of the discussion was a family which had been allocated a house there. The transcript ran:

'But they're *interlaupers*.'
'Naw — they're *jiners*.'
Consult a Paisley dictionary for elucidation.

- And a reader who worked for Falkirk District Council recalled a committee chairman complaining that his colleagues were *flogging a wild goose*.

'Strangely enough,' he says, 'I knew exactly what he meant.'

HIGHLAND Region councillors were wrong-footed when Caithness member and former tabloid journalist Bill Mowat introduced a special motion on a football topic. He asked the council to congratulate the Faroe Islands for beating Austria in the European Championships. 'After all,' he said, 'they speak the language we used in Caithness before we spoke English.' Despite mystification in the council chamber, the motion was agreed. In English.

DESIGNER Marxism was alive and well and living in Edinburgh City

Chambers. The Labour Group administration officer found it necessary to send a circular round her flock to look for a missing 'six-hole punch'. This is, of course, an essential tool for users of Filofaxes and other yuppie-style 'personal organisers'.

The circular read: 'The punch appears to have gone astray and I am led to believe that one of the councillors 'borrowed' it. I would be grateful if the punch could be returned as soon as possible so that all councillors can have access to it.'

The vision comes to mind of anguished left-wingers, with piles of loose paper on their desks, overcome by personal disorganisation. However, the memo did the trick and the punch turned up within 24 hours, handed over with an apology by an absent-minded Labour member. Much hooting from the old-fashioned working-class lefties of course.

MOTHERWELL district councillors were finding it hard to escape that reputation for junketing overseas. Tut, tut — an unwarranted suggestion even cropped up during a meeting of the COSLA Labour Group, discussing the situation of the late lamented Ravenscraig steel works.

A motion from Charles Gray, of Strathclyde Region, was on the table: but who should second it? There was nobody there from Motherwell, the appropriate district council.

Then came the laconic suggestion by Bill Derby, of Dundee: 'Maybe, they could second it by satellite link-up?' It pains us to report that the meeting erupted in laughter.

IN THE life of the local politician, there are moments to be cherished. Such an event occurred when a gaggle of Edinburgh planning committee members set out by bus on one of their periodical sorties, to inspect the *loci* of various development projects.

In this solemn pursuit of their responsibilities, they were to be found stumbling around a back garden in Ellen's Glen Road, Liberton, where a poll-taxpayer had sought permission to erect a house extension.

A city official produced the plans, drawn up at no meagre expense by a qualified architect. Heads bent over the sheet of paper and lips pursed as the city's supreme planning mandarins grappled with the aesthetic implications of somebody's sun-lounge.

It was at this point that the back door opened. The man who stood there asked the planning committee what they thought they were doing in his back garden. The planning committee explained.

The man replied that they needn't bother themselves: he had applied for planning permission at the beginning of the year and had become tired of waiting. He had sold the house and was preparing to move out. Thank you and goodbye.

It was a chastened planning committee that climbed back into its bus.

S U R P R I Z E S

HERE'S a yarn from the exciting interface between the state services and the punters they serve. We are in the accident and emergency unit at Edinburgh Royal Infirmary. A young man walks in for medical assistance. Patiently, he answers the usual questions about name, address, blood-group, daytime phone number etc.

Then comes the big question: what's wrong with him? 'Promise you won't laugh,' he begs and raises a hand to which is attached a telephone receiver and a dangling length of cord.

The story was that he'd been in a call box when some friends — well, ex-friends — smeared superglue over the phone. As a result, he had been tethered to the phone for more than an hour before he was cut free. He was last seen being led away by a medico who planned to perform some magic with solvents.

THERE was another stage-farce situation at Edinburgh Royal Infirmary when two Lothian councillors dropped in for first-hand observation of the pressures on the emergency unit.

As councillors William Herald and Donald Gorrie were being shown round by consultants, there was a flurry of muttered orders and some quick movement. Just before the two fact-finders were ushered into a consulting room, a recently-deceased person was swiftly wheeled out.

CURIOUS fact — stumbled into as Highland Distilleries pored over a survey of the drinks market. Two-thirds of the Benedictine liqueur drunk in the UK goes down throats in South Gloucestershire.

This strange taste can apparently be traced back to the First World War, when a South Gloucestershire regiment was billeted in a Benedictine monastery. Hmm.

AN ironical development in post-Wall Germany. East German Air Force officers took to telephoning their counterparts in the West to ask if there were any jobs going. According to senior sources at NATO headquarters in Brussels, the callers included pilots who would probably rather be at the controls of a new Tornado than an elderly MiG.

There were also cases of East German soldiers who left for the West, calling at barracks and recruiting offices and asking to sign up for what was until then the 'other side' in the Cold War.

One NATO military figure, said: 'I think we should definitely keep them on file. They would be ideal for our verification teams, sent in to monitor arms cuts. They would know just what to look for and where everything is stored.'

Elementary, my dear Le Carré.

A LONDON-BASED public relations company advertised for a PR and marketing manager, replete with all the usual skills. All hopefuls were invited to write to:

Nicholas J. Bunkum

MORE from the department of appropriate names:

- The manager of a branch of the Royal Bank of Scotland in Ayr was a Mr Clydesdale.
- The head of religious education at an Edinburgh school was a Mr Priestly.
- The 'learning difficulties' tutor at the same establishment was a Mrs Blott.
- Those interested in the Chinese 'Year of the Sheep' were invited to contact the Hong Kong office in London and ask for a Miss Lam.
- An application for an extension of drinking hours was lodged in Dumfries by a publican named David Tippler.
- The director of Marriage Counselling Scotland was Mrs Frances Love.
- The director of the Turkish Tourist Office was Mustafa Turkmen.
- The Meat and Livestock Commission announced the appointment of a new marketing manager: Christopher Lamb.
- Among the DoE boffins looking into the problem of pesticides polluting streams and rivers was Ray Otter.
- Lothian Region had two buyers eminently suited to making deals: F. C. Clinch and E. Clinch.
- A shop selling bric-à-brac in a certain West Highland ferry port took the name 'Oban Sesame'.
- We refuse to take the word of a reader claiming that the Russian author who first drew attention to the dangers of smoking was an Ivan Offalkov.

EAT too much, did we? A touch of the old flatulence? Never mind, this could be the answer:

FROM the Diary's committed staff of Notice Board Readers spread out right across the country:

- 'The special Chinese Evening scheduled for 2 February has been cancelled, as it clashes with the Welsh rugby international.' (The Edinburgh University Staff Club.)
- 'Children are welcome provided they do not approach the bar or *disturd* other customers.' (Hotel in Sutherland.)
- Sign (in English) at Chinese takeaway in Lanark: 'Open seven days (except Monday).'

- Sign in the window of an antiques shop in Coniston, in the Lake District: 'We buy anything old — except parents and in-laws, particularly in-laws.' Sounds as if there's a wealth of bitter experience behind that proclamation.
- The Oxfam shop in Morningside, Edinburgh, seemed to be concerned with famine relief for the world's most populous nation. A poster in the window saying: 'Special Appeal for China . . . ' added: ' . . . and Glassware.'
- Spotted on the bar menu at Misty Isle Hotel, Dunvegan, Skye: 'Poll Tax Pie — fishy, half-baked and hard to swallow — £243.00.'
- From a St Andrews student noticeboard: 'Talk on Oxfam *Hungry for Change* Fast. Chaplaincy 1 p.m. Hot lunch provided.'
- At Wormit Primary School, a pupil doing a Second World War project described the 'Evacuation from Dunkeld'.
- Notice in a Fife antique shop window: 'Pensioner Wanted'.
- The *Sunday Pewspaper* of St Peter's Episcopal Church, Lutton Place, Edinburgh, optimistically invited its readers to contribute to a 'cakes and brandy' stall.
- The Royal Lyceum Theatre, Edinburgh, sent out a leaflet offering season-ticket holders an exclusive car-parking facility. Motorists were told: 'No more searching for a parking space. Instead, you could be relaxing in one of the theatre's bars . . . '
- A Glasgow newspaper referred to Michael Howard as 'the Unemployment Secretary'.
- From a hotel bar in Tarbert, Argyll: 'Corner House Sweep: Have you paid? Subscribers missing two payments in a row will be scrubbed.'
- We further noted the latest in car rear-window stickers: 'Love the grandchildren. Wish we had them first.'

WE are indebted to the West Highland Free Press for this Byzantine mystery, posed in its advertising columns:

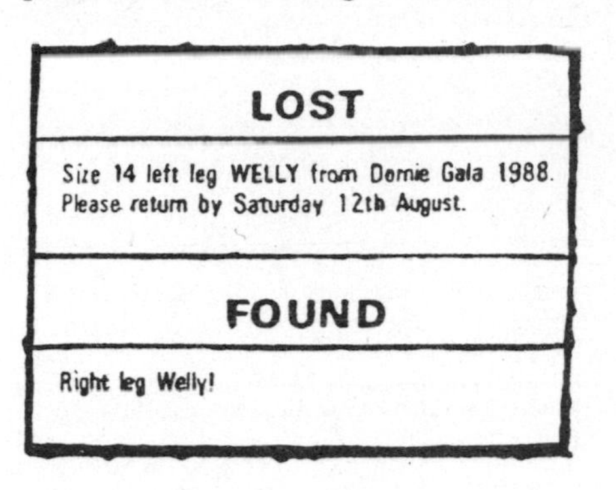
LOST

Size 14 left leg WELLY from Dornie Gala 1988. Please return by Saturday 12th August.

FOUND

Right leg Welly!

QUITE irresistible offer from the *Observer* gardening catalogue — and it cost only £12.50:

3	Crap Apple Tree

A GENIAL octogenarian was in the Chalmers Hospital, Edinburgh, for an operation which entailed her being 'opened' down the middle from chest to tummy. When two surgeons visited her next day to check her progress, she greeted them with the question: 'Which one of you filleted me?'

She didn't get an answer, and it was only as she was being released that she learned her operation had been performed by a Mr Haddock.

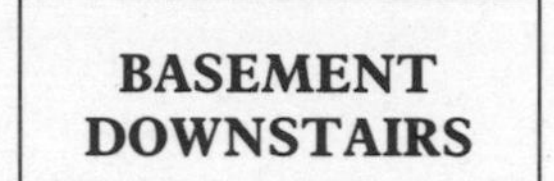

IF YOU think this notice in Glasgow Royal Infirmary states the obvious, you would be quite right. But it's been there for many years, and it is regularly repainted.

Apparently, a former administrator was so fed up with medical students asking the way to the basement that he had the sign put up as a joke. Now it has become part of the hospital tradition and any attempt to remove it would cause an uproar. Also, medical students would probably start asking the way to the basement again.

National Schizophrenia Fellowship
2 ASSISTANT DIRECTORS
£18,000 - £20,000

A very worthy charity, the NSF. But perhaps they should have put in a clause discouraging people from applying for both jobs?

THESE Glasgow pensioners were very impressed by the coach driver who took them on their outing through the Scottish Borders.

He drove very carefully along the narrow roads, giving them plenty of time to admire the scenery.

They seemed particularly interested in the fields full of cattle and sheep. The driver slowed down frequently to give straying sheep the right of way.

When the coach stopped at Moffat, the grateful passengers invited their driver to join them for high tea. As the orders were placed for steak pies, gammon etc, the driver was heard demanding: 'A cheese salad for me, please. I don't believe in killing and eating animals.'

Sudden silence. A passenger then explained that this tour had been booked by the 400-year-old Incorporation of Fleshers of Glasgow, dedicated to maintaining standards in the meat trade (its curious motto: 'Thou hast put all things under his feet . . . cattle'). His passengers were all retired butchers and their wives.

The return journey was quick — and straight along the motorway.

Yours sincerely

Robin Hood

R Hood
Crime Prevention Publicity

THE toast of a Summer Ball in Edinburgh were two second-year students at Heriot-Watt University business school. The theme of the event was fruit and flowers: but not being keen on fancy dress, they compromised by wearing flowery waistcoats with their dinner suits, and a flower in their buttonholes.

Their parents were aghast. These things must be done properly, they said. One mother, a legendary party-giver, took the boys to a costume hirer to be kitted out with the full works.

So on the great night, they turned up in spectacular outfits. One was dressed as a pineapple and the other, in a green leotard covered with green balloons, as a bunch of grapes.

All the other men, of course, were in . . . dinner jackets with a flower in the lapel, and floral bow ties.

The students, however, were the stars of the show. When Bunch of Grapes arrived home in the small hours, he'd been left with only two balloons intact, for the sake of decency.

IT'S interesting that technology which can send messages round the world in fractions of a second still can't cope properly with a gathering of farmers. The National Farmers' Union of Scotland seems to be particularly bedevilled with microphones that reduce fine oratory to a squeak, a squawk or a buzzing in the ears (although some cynics suggest this can be achieved without modern amplification).

Events reached a new pitch at the union's council meeting in the MacRobert Pavilion at Ingliston, near Edinburgh. After the usual problems of adjusting the main microphones, and queries over whether the circulating mike needed new batteries, things seemed to have settled down. Then, as president John Ross answered a question, a microphone to his left burst into independent action and was heard to demand: 'Can I speak to the manager, please. Yes, as soon as possible.'

The farmers were stunned into unaccustomed silence; a microphone with such a peremptory manner was clearly something to be admired.

Then the mike (which seemed to be picking up phone messages) boomed out again: 'Whatever you do, don't flush the toilet!' The farmers now couldn't contain themselves, in a manner of speaking.

It took real restraint to return to the problems of land set-aside and marketing premiums.

OVERHEARD in Valvona & Crolla's Edinburgh food emporium, where hungry Italophiles queue studiously every Saturday for Mediterranean comestibles:

Punter: 'Why are you playing those '50s tapes on the louspeaker? It's usually Pavarotti.'

Assistant: 'Ah. We didn't think it would be appropriate to play Luciano at the moment. He's on a diet.'

AS summer approaches, hotel life gets more interesting. At Edinburgh's Sheraton, food and drink manager Colin Bennett was startled to hear a Spanish room-service waitress announce that she had to deliver something to Fred Astaire. The manager was pretty sure that Fred Astaire (1899-1987) was not actually staying at the hotel.

Further close questioning solved the mystery. The order to room-service had been placed by Freddie Starr, the comedian.

There was drama, too, in the lobby when a group of ten Japanese gentlemen were found in animated conversation with the concierge. One of them was holding a small trout, weighing less than a pound. He had caught it. He was very proud. None of his companions had caught anything. The successful angler insisted that the fish should be cooked by the chef and divided up between the ten of them.

This was eventually done: but the chef (performing his own miracle of the loaves and fishes) secretly added fresh trout from the hotel's own supply so that nobody would end up completely ravenous.

PRESUMABLY they have had enough of deranged journalists under their feet. This vacancy at the Campaign for Nuclear Disarmament suggests that they are going to try something else:

HERE'S a curious medical case-history from the *New Scientist* — which points out that doctors always like to report successes. And this success happened many years ago. The patient was an asthma sufferer. Symptoms were worsening and his life was threatened.

But this patient was a smoker. His doctor — Dr William Frankland, vice-chairman of the National Asthma Campaign — refused to let smokers return to his clinic until they had given up the weed. He persuaded this patient to do so. Result: the patient recovered – another triumph for medical science.

The paper reports that Frankland now has a niggling doubt. 'His patient was, at the time, the deputy chairman of Iraq's Revolutionary Command Council. Yes, that's him — the noted Iraqi author and statesman, Saddam Hussein.'

NOBODY fell asleep, apparently, when Glasgow anaesthetist Dr Richard Wolfson addressed an Edinburgh Rotary Club lunch. Instead, his listeners were in stitches. (End of bad joke section.)

His best effort was to recall a spoonerism perpetrated by a young man, handing over a coffee percolator he'd bought for a friend as a wedding present. 'I hope you find this perky copulator very useful,' he stammered.

FIVE English fortune-tellers abandoned their 'psychic tour' of Ireland after their crystal balls, tarot cards and other impedimenta of the trade were stolen from their parked car outside a Dublin guest house. One said it would be difficult to recover their property now they had no crystal ball to help them.

Another, Margaret Pickering from Hull, said: 'We were aware something was about to happen, but we did not know what'.

ANYTHING the Russkies can do, the Yanks can do better. And that seems to include Glasnost. This must be why we found this entry in the London phone book:

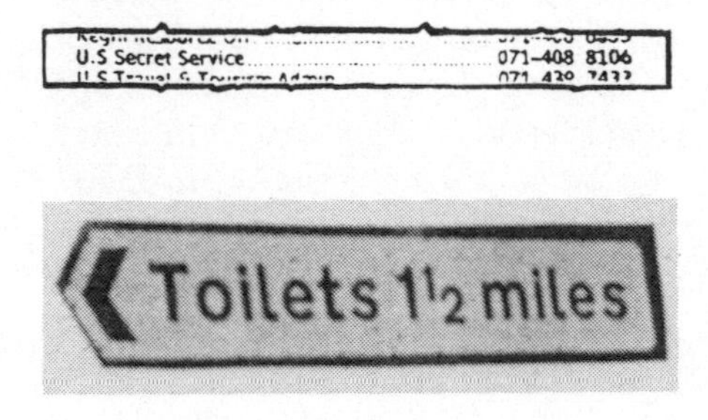
U.S Secret Service 071-408 8106

OUR occasional series on silly signs flushed out an amazing number of enthusiasts for the genre.

The sign above is beside a footpath in the Borders, and must have doubled up many walkers with dismay. It's at St Mary's Loch, quite close to Tibbie Shiel's Inn.

NOT too long after the Conservative Government showed its used-car-salesman mentality by selling off 'cherished' number plates, there was this strange sighting in the streets of Edinburgh. It was a vehicle with the registration plate, ULB 1 ('You'll Be One').

Ironically enough, the number plate was fixed to a hearse.

WHO could fail to be moved by the fond farewell which *Alcohol Concern* magazine gave to the director of Action on Alcohol Abuse, leaving the agency after 12 years:

> Goodbye Don
> Alcohol abuse without Don Steele will seem strangely quiet, somewhat duller, and a little less fun . . .

THERE was a bit of a scare for Shell persons when they invaded the tiny Shetland isle of Fetlar (population 90) for a doomwatch practice-run. This was 'Operation Clearwater', a three-day exercise in which they assumed there had been a fracture in the pipeline which runs offshore.

As the imaginary oil gurgled messily into the sea, they tested their emergency procedures. They flew local man John Coutts — editor of Fetlar's community newspaper — to the command post at Brae where he recorded the activities on videotape.

But Greenpeace activists had heard about the event (maybe they read about it in the Diary), and decided to join in. They did this by phoning Shell rather persistently and asking what they were going to do about the seals and other wildlife which were becoming theoretically coated with imaginary oil.

The oil persons were becoming a little annoyed with this distraction when their video operator started to feel the heat and pulled off his jersey. There he stood, resplendent in a Greenpeace T-shirt. As security men closed in ominously, it was explained that he wasn't actually a Greenpeace soldier; he just liked their semmits.

He carried on filming, although he may just have been kept under slightly more scrutiny than before . . .

THEY call it education updating, and when retired schools inspector Sandy Jeffrey addressed a seminar on this subject in Glasgow, the term came curiously true.

He started off by observing that 350 years ago 'to the very day', King Charles I was taken to Whitehall and had his head chopped off. (Sound of meshing brain cogs in the audience.) 'That can't be right,' observed a female voice. 'Surely he was beheaded in 1649.' (Moment of slight confusion on the platform.)

After a break for tea, Sandy returned with an apology. It had been the Marquess of Montrose, not Charles I. And it had been Edinburgh, not London. The bit about the head coming off was, however, entirely accurate.

RELIGIOUS education has its moments too. A Catholic priest taking a class in Liverpool started off by asking the little darlings to list the Ten Commandments: but after 'Thou shalt not kill' and 'Thou shalt not steal', the pupils became lost in a sort of mental Sinai Desert.

The best they could come up with was 'Thou shalt be kind to other people', which was at least an inspired guess. But after they branched out into 'Thou shalt not take drugs' and 'Thou shalt not bunk off school', he called a halt to the exercise. Appropriately half of the class was absent at the time.

HAS Edinburgh's Cameron Toll shopping centre become the new Lourdes? A reader who managed to find a spot in the crowded carpark was locking up when he saw a yuppie-style cabriolet drive into a space reserved for disabled drivers. Out climbed the motorist, who clearly didn't qualify for the facility.

At that moment a voice carried clearly across the carpark from where two labourers were working. 'Look, Jim,' it roared. 'Another bloody miracle!'

The driver strode away with a nonchalance that was belied by the reddening of his ears.

THE *Irish Times* received a telex from the Met Office which warned: 'General Situation: A cold front is moving erotically southwards over Ireland.' In Dublin, people looked hopefully from their windows on the Monday morning in question, to find the day bright and breezy, but no sexier than usual.

WHEN the *Irish Times* and the *Times Higher Education Supplement* passed on howlers from examination papers, the first three had a particularly Irish resonance:

'Planning can have the effect of containing people in grottos; Luther was born a Protestant . . . later, he converted to Christianity; and Pascal gambolled on the existence of God.'

This one, however, is an all-round collector's item: 'Heracles is often depicted as wholly naked, and in these circumstances one can often see his attributes laid on one side or hanging from a rock.'

But there was worse ahead for examinees who took the biology paper for the Irish Leaving Certificate. A note read: 'All students should be sterilised before starting a microbiology experiment.'

SIR IAN MacGREGOR — the man who dramatically emerged from a car during the miners' strike with a polythene bag over his head — was once caught out without one of those useful accessories. Never did he need one more.

The former Coal Board hatchet-man had been addressing an NFU dinner in Peebles and set off in the morning to catch the 8 a.m. Edinburgh-Heathrow shuttle and a connection for New York.

He was driven by the NFU's Judy Nichols, using her own car. The car had just been fitted with new tyres: that's the end of the good news. The bad news is that it suffered a puncture atop the blasted heath north of Peebles, in lashing rain.

For some time, Judy and her passenger struggled in vain to free a tight nut on the wheel, but had to give in. Along came a handy lorry, and the driver gave the saturated travellers a hurl as far as Penicuik, where they could hire a taxi.

The next stage of the journey must have been the most uncomfortable ride of MacGregor's career. The taxi-driver turned out to be an ex-miner, made redundant from Bilston Glen Colliery at the time of Sir Ian's turbulent reign. He knew perfectly well who his passenger was (what ex-miner wouldn't?) but nevertheless made sure he caught his plane.

And what next? After a hectic round of engagements in the United States, Sir Ian headed for Czechoslovakia *where he is to advise on the development of the mining industry* (our italics).

That taxi-driving ex-miner might have a lot to answer for.

MEDITATION became a trifle difficult at the Edinburgh Dharma Study Group, as those seeking the Buddhist path waited for the next tap on the door.

The first knock came when the students had been seated silently on their cushions for about 15 minutes, breathing the incense-perfumed air and *following their breath as it went out and dissolved, connecting with their hearts*. Someone could be heard entering the room behind the Japanese-style cloth partition, and coughing discreetly to attract attention; a student went to investigate.

The meditators heard a conversation which began: 'Excuse me, is this — eh — a massage place? My pal saw the sign so I thought I'd drop in . . . ' As the student gave the caller a short homily on *mindfulness* and *food-sharing*, group-meditation was temporarily interrupted for serious laughter-control.

The other knock came when a monk was leading the 'Theravada' group in some silent contemplation. Enter three schoolboys. They responded to the whispered suggestion that they could come in if they took their shoes off and didn't say a word. One of them was more cautious than the others. He inquired loudly: 'It's no' paedophiles, is it?' It took some time for the bad vibes to dissipate.

However, these Dharma types are resilient. They had already survived the challenge of meditating while the sounds of *Brookside* could be heard filtering down from the upstairs flat.

WHEN library books go missing, the efforts made to retrieve them can vary from threats of court action on the one hand to a general amnesty for offenders on the other. But what happens when the books turn up but the library itself appears to be lost?

An advertisement curiously headed 'Lost/Found?' appeared in the *Library Association Record*.

The advertiser said he 'would be pleased to receive any inquiries regarding two volumes of Archbold's *Criminal Practice and Pleading* which had come into his possession.'

And who was this paragon, prepared to go such lengths to return these volumes to their rightful shelves?

He was in fact, the library officer at HM Prison, Stafford.

EDINBURGH & BORDERS Hunt Saboteur Group decided to switch tactics one weekend. Instead of picketing a foxhunting meet they turned up outside an Edinburgh hotel to picket the Linlithgow and Stirlingshire Hunt Ball.

Who knows what plans they had. To lay a false scent from the ladies' powder room to the bar? To drown out the band with duck calls?

In the event it didn't matter: for after hanging around outside the hotel for some time, the luckless saboteurs discovered that the ball had been cancelled due to poor ticket sales.

Then occurred one of those delightful coincidences which add colour to the protester's life. Up drew a coach with the name 'William Hunter of Loanhead' emblazoned on the side, together with the company symbol of a huntsman in full fig. It had come to collect a party from the hotel — but for the saboteurs, it was a somewhat belated 'View halloo'.

One could be heard wondering whether this was a subtle form of provocation, but the coach was allowed to proceed, without a placard or epithet flaunted.

THE most unexpected people do a spot of part-time taxi-driving. This was discovered by Jimmy Grant, of Dalmeny, a regular at the Forth Bar in South Queensferry. When he feels it's time to go home, the bar staff phone for a taxi. 'That's your cab, Jimmy,' called out a regular, seeing a car draw up outside. So Jimmy left the bar and climbed into the back of the smart Mercedes.

The driver, who was at a nearby cash dispenser, didn't expect a fare in the back seat when he returned. 'What are you doing there?' asked the puzzled driver — Stephen Hendry, the world snooker champion, who lives in the town.

'Oh, it's you son,' said Jimmy lamely. 'I thought it was my taxi.' Displaying the *sangfroid* which has conquered a hundred opponents, young Stephen just drove Jimmy home anyway, free of charge. And no tip either.

POLITICS

MARGARET THATCHER was returned to the ranks of the Scottish Anti-Poll Tax Federation, concealed in a black plastic bag. But this, of course, was the effigy of Maggie which the federation used to parade through the streets, in a perspex coffin, during their rallies against the poll tax.

It was a dummy constructed by art students from stuffed tights with a Maggie mask, and dressed in a vivid blue two-piece suit.

According to anti-poll tax campaigner Tommy Sheridan, the effigy and its coffin were stolen from the group's offices in London Street, Glasgow, while everyone's back was turned.

The thief discarded the coffin, but the dummy of Maggie seemed to inspire him with a spirit of free enterprise. He discovered that if he took it round the local pubs, there were plenty of Glaswegians who were willing to pay him 20p to give it a kick.

But this form of entertainment clearly had a limited appeal, and the effigy was later abandoned in a back street. It was found there by a woman, who recognised it immediately, and returned it to its home.

THERE is a 'Tory Street' in Wellington, the New Zealand capital. But the rival North Island city of Auckland has a street where there will be no U-turns, no back-seat driving, and which goes on, and on, and on. This is it:

THERE are those among us who feel, at times, that the Keystone Cops have nothing on the House of Commons. Perhaps this feeling might be strengthened by a procedural episode, reported by *Hansard* in its usual splendidly po-faced fashion. Our own essential background notes are added in italics:

Mr Frank Cook (Lab., Stockton North): Further to that point of order, Mr Deputy Speaker . . .

Mr Deputy Speaker (Harold Walker, Lab., Doncaster Central): Order. The Hon. Gentleman will cover himself properly.

No — Mr Cook's zip is not undone. He has simply overlooked the convention that any MP wishing to raise a Point of Order during a division must remain seated and wear a hat. A collapsible opera hat is kept in the chamber for this purpose.

Mr Cook (seated and covered): Would you have the courtesy, Sir, to explain to the House why hon. Members must endure the inverse convention of sitting here with a hat on while you can answer points of order standing in the normal way with your head bare? Is this not a means of making hon. Members look ridiculous and deterring them from raising points of order during a division?

Mr Deputy Speaker: The hon. Gentleman must not hold me responsible for the conventions, traditions and Standing Orders of the House. That is a matter for the House. And when the hon. Gentleman talks about bald heads — well, with respect . . .

Despite the clear inference by Mr Walker, Mr Cook is not actually bald. He has had his head shaved for charity, and Mr Deputy Speaker is making a humorous reference to his gleaming skull. Mr Walker, on the other hand, happens to be thinning on top.

Mr Cook: Further to that point of order, Mr Deputy Speaker. I did not mean to imply that I held you responsible . . .

Mr Deputy Speaker: I would not dream of trying to explain to the House the reasons for our Standing Orders. (*In this case for 'Standing Orders' read 'Sitting Orders'*.) If the hon. Gentleman was suggesting that on future occasions I should be appropriately covered, he might be prepared to have a whip round for a wig for me.

The beauty of this exchange is that we never discover what point of order Mr Cook originally had in mind.

IT was Norman Tebbit who postulated that the true test of 'British' nationality was to support the English cricket team.

Something equally weird cropped up at a Glasgow conference on nationalism, organised by What's Left, the straggling remnants of what used to be the Scottish Communist Party, and joined by activists of many political flavours

In an attempt to get to the nub of the matter, a small grey-haired lady began to question the chairwoman, Joyce MacMillan, about how she was identified on her passport. 'Are you Scottish or British?' demanded the Wendy Wood of Kelvinside.

Before an answer could be given, a wag from the audience translated this into a Scottishness litmus test which may stand for all time: 'Do you eat haggis suppers or fish suppers?'

THE Scottish Conservatives continued down the hearts and minds trail, using every possible social occasion to *get the message across*. But we couldn't work out whether this report of such a event in the *Galloway News* constituted fair comment or a misprint:

Dalbeattie
CHEESE AND WIND — We must stand by our principles and retain our faith in the Conservative philosophy said Sir Donald

IT was Mrs Thatcher (was it not?) who used cricketing metaphors to say she would fight to retain the Tory leadership. Didn't help much. But nevertheless, the technique was adopted by Labour MP Alf Morris (Wythenshawe), who told a Commons committee:

'The feeling on this side of the committee is that, as the debate proceeded, the minister was bowled out and ought to have left the crease. While we are not totally satisfied with the umpiring of the committee . . . ' (Hon Members: 'Oh!')

But from the chair, Norman Hogg delivered the following googly: 'I never respond to cricketing metaphors, because I am a Scot and cricket is a game that the English play badly.' Howzat?

THERE'S nothing more fruitful for a diarist than a gloves-off by-election. And so . . .

• OBSERVERS at the Kincardine & Deeside hustings were fascinated by the hard evidence which the competing parties produced to show that they, and they alone, could expect to inherit the seat.

Hoping to hold the seat, the Tories offered a comparison between the 1986 and the 1990 regional election results to show an impressive increase in their share of the vote.

The Lib Dems presented just the 1990 regional results to draw attention to their second place, only 4 per cent behind the Tories, as well as two district by-elections which they won.

Labour seemed to prefer current countrywide opinion poll results which showed them ahead of the Tories, with the Lib Dems nowhere.

For different reasons, the SNP placed high credence on the most recent result for the North-East Scotland constituency in the European Parliament.

But for inventive originality, top marks should go to the Scottish Greens. They were spotlighting results from an election for Oslo Distric Council, conducted under proportional representation. In this poll, a significant block of women members was elected — and so, ladies, why shouldn't it happen here? (It didn't.)

• THE scene is Kincorth, in by-election poppin' Kincardine and Deeside. Everywhere, political activists are on the knocker, and one MP rings a doorbell, adjusts his smile, and finds the door opened by the lady of the house.

Behind her, the place is ablaze with colourful blooms, like a small flower show.

'Wonderful,' he says enthusiastically, 'superb show!' To his surprise, the poor voter bursts into tears.

'They're from my man's funeral,' she sobs. 'I buried him last week.'

We will draw a veil over the hapless politician's stammered attempt at damage-control.

• THE candidates were not short of local and national issues to grapple with. Nevertheless, they were bowled a googly in a fax sent to all competing parties by the *Pink Paper*, 'the national newspaper for lesbians and gay men'.

It asked all candidates to state their position on homosexual rights, including 'discrimination against homosexuals in the armed forces'. Naturally, dubious jokes were circulating: even the suggestion that this had something to do with 'the proposed amalgamation of the Gay Gordons with the Queen's Own Highlanders'.

• HI-TECH journos flooding into Stonehaven for the various party press conferences were slightly discommoded. They discovered that due to some geological aberration, their *poserphones* were unable to contact base.

What a shame. They were unable to relay back the priceless information from the Scottish Conservative Media Guide concerning the old fishing village of Findon, a haven of the haddock. 'Findon,' says the guide sonorously, 'once famed for its finnan baddies . . . '

• LAST call for Kincardine and Deeside. Edinburgh Lib Dem candidate Devin Scobie, up in the constituency to hustle votes, noticed with interest that the Tory Party leaflets were printed at a prophetic address: 12 Back Wynd. He filed this away mentally for future use — until noticing that his own party's literature came from 4 Crooked Lane.

• THE Monmouth by-election was supposed to be an opportunity for the Government to test the temperature of the electorate before deciding on a date for the big match in 1992. But it also gave at least one Welsh voter a chance to try out a new hustings survival technique.

This by-election was seen by many parties and the loony fringe as an important set-piece. Manifestos, printed promises and declarations of intent poured through the Monmouth letterboxes in a torrent. It was too much for our experimental voter, who placed an open bin-bag beside his garden gate with a notice reading: 'Please deposit all election leaflets here.'

One Labour Party helper did just that. But he had been watched from behind the net curtains, and the voter came running down the path to congratulate him. 'You are the first person to use the bag,' he said. 'Which party do you represent?' The helper said it was Labour. 'Then you have my vote,' said this original thinker: and as we now know, Labour went on to win the seat. Hm.

SIR RUSSELL JOHNSTON told his fellow Lib Dems the sad yet heartening tale of auld Sandy, a constituent in Fort William and a 'Liberal' all his life.

Sandy was in hospital — but worse, he had changed his allegiance and joined the Tories. The MP called at the hospital, where he found Sandy 'no weel at a'.'

Sir R.: 'I'm sorry to hear that Sandy. But what's this about you joining the Conservatives?'

Sandy: 'Ah'm, afraid it's true. Ah dinna think ah'm gonny get oota here. So it's better they lose one than we do.'

SOME interesting motions were listed for debate at the Labour Party's annual conference in Blackpool. One concerned the control or banning of 'dangerous breeds' of dogs. Aptly enough, this canine resolution came from the Constituency Labour Party at Barking.

FULL of merry quips and subtle jokes they are, these right-wing strategists of the Adam Smith Institute. Their plan for reforming local government in Scotland, punningly titled *Shedding a Tier*, had on its cover a picture of two playing cards, like so:

The 'joker' card, in fact, bore a silhouette of dear old Adam himself. But why choose a nine of diamonds? The think-tank commander of the ASI, Dr Madsen Pirie, chose to be obscure about this, telling us merely: 'I suppose various people will read what they like into it. All we are trying to suggest by using playing cards is a "new deal" for Scotland.'

This, to use Foreign Office phraseology is 'totally unacceptable'. The nine of diamonds is, of course, popularly known as 'the curse of Scotland', and the Diary learns that the decision to use it as a cover illustration was dreamed up by Adam Smithites during a session in Methuselah's wine bar, near New Scotland Yard.

There are seven possible reasons why the card is regarded as Scotland's curse. The most significant ones are that the infamous 'Butcher', the Duke of Cumberland, used the back of the card to write his merciless orders after Culloden; and that there was a link with the arms of Dalrymple, Earl of Stair, who was loathed for his part in the Massacre of Glencoe.

There were hints that the Adam Smith Institute believed the Labour-dominated local authorities are the curse of Scotland; but then they would, wouldn't they?

THE Conservative Party beavered away busily in the wake of the Representation of the People Act 1989, under which more Britons living abroad were entitled to vote in Westminster elections. James Spicer, the Tory MP for Dorset West and chairman of the 'Conservatives Abroad' organisation, estimated that around two million expatriate voters were there to be wooed. But a letter from 'Conservatives Abroad' led to some hilarity in Scottish political circles. It said: 'We calculate that anyone who left England for permanent residence abroad after 10 October 1970, will qualify for the 1991–1992 register as an overseas elector.' Lots of those who left 'England', of course, settled in Scotland. Was this a slip of the computer, or (to adapt a Tory phrase) was Scotland to get Conservatism through the back door?

MORE Tory news: We heard of an absolutely fascinating piece of research being conducted at a high level at Tory Scottish Central Office, in Leith.

Some months before, the staff of around 20 moved into the former Leith Provident building. Their neighbours were the Scottish Equitable Life Assurance Society, with about 200 employees. Yet the building managers discovered that the Tories were using more toilet rolls than Scottish Equitable. In fact, nearly double the number.

Inquiries were conducted discreetly by the Tory office manager, whose first task was to check back through the records to see how many toilet rolls the party used to get through in its former offices at Chester Street.

We never learned the outcome of this research — or saw the psychologist's report. Pity.

AS A drinking den, the House of Commons is notably more sober than it once was. This is the conclusion of Professor Alan Thompson, of Heriot-Watt University, and former Labour MP for Dunfermline. He wrote in *Edinburgh Medicine*: 'I do not think there is a serious problem of alcoholism in British public life, although there are no doubt problems of individual excess. There is no bigotry against reasonable drinking in public life, but a politician who revived the drinking habits of the Earl of Chatham would not long survive as Prime Minister.'

This was a reference to William Pitt, the 18th-century PM, who managed to restrict his drinking to three bottles of port a day. To be fair, the bottles were smaller then.

Professor Thompson recalled that Herbert Asquith, who was sometimes unsteady on his feet, earned the nickname 'Squiffy'. But he didn't believe Winston Churchill matched up to his reputation as a heavy drinker, although he cultivated the image in later life to annoy the teetotal Field Marshal Montgomery.

'Changing attitudes to drinking in politics reflect changing attitudes in the community,' he wrote. 'Nobody now shares the uncritical view of earlier centuries in the therapeutic value of drink.'

The best tale was of Lord Palmerston, who eventually restricted his drinking to champagne but, at the age of 79, did not cut down on his sexual exploits. He is alleged to have committed adultery with a young Irish widow, Mrs O'Kane, leading to the reputed remark by his Tory opponent, Disraeli, 'I know she was Kane, but was Palmerston Abel?'

Asked whether the scandal should be used as an election issue, Disraeli responded: 'Certainly not. He'd sweep the country.'

MICHAEL FORSYTH can't say he wasn't warned. As the former Scottish health minister lay abed a while ago with throbbing head and blocked sinuses, his mind may have gone back to a letter he had received only days previously.

It was from Graeme Millar, chairman of the Pharmaceutical General Council (Scotland), warning of the dangers of a flu epidemic and urging the minister to ensure plentiful supplies of vaccine were available.

Health education in action, you could say — and very prompt too.

THE late Norman Buchan, the one-off MP and enthusiast for Scottish life, wrote many songs — but never a campaign song for himself. He once wrote a beauty which helped Judith Hart win the South Lanark seat in 1959. But asked why he hadn't produced one for his own campaigning, he said he didn't want to risk it: his surname had 'too many rhyming possibilities'.

This was actually borne out in the 1987 General Election campaign. One of his supporters, who had been shouting slogans through a loudhailer in a council scheme in Johnstone, was approached by the police. 'We've had complaints from some pensioners,' they said. 'Somebody has been shouting obscenities at them through a loudhailer.'

'Who, me?'

'Well, what *were* you shouting?'

'Vote Buchan Labour,' said the mystified young man.

Norman's agent had to read the Riot Act and forbid the use of that particular phrase. But when the Tories were returned to power, Norman observed philosophically that the slogan the Johnstone pensioners thought they'd heard should have been shouted from the rooftops.

MICHAEL FORSYTH'S 'promotion' from the Scottish Office was a severe setback to the Diary. So let us remember the good times . . .

THERE was a small outbreak of psychological warfare when Michael Forsyth addressed the conference of the Rating & Valuation Association in Aviemore.

Like most politicians, the Scottish Tory Party chairman had left the writing of his speech to the last moment, and he scribbled some notes as he was being driven north from his home in Aberfoyle.

But he was rather short of notepaper: so he jotted his thoughts down on the back of one of those cheeky Tory posters which read: 'Donald, whaur's your figures?' — taunting the Shadow Scottish Secretary over the fog surrounding his roof tax.

Forsyth went to the rostrum and delivered his poll tax peroration. But he had discovered (to his delight, we suspect) that the speaker scheduled to follow him to the rostrum was none other than D. Dewar. So the Tory chairman 'accidentally' left his notes on the lectern.

Wrong side up, of course . . .

OFF with the old! On with the new! When the Scottish Conservative Party launched its new, exciting logo at a press conference in Edinburgh, chairman Michael Forsyth asked reporters (rather drily, some thought) if they noticed the improvement. The old one is on the left, the new one on the right:

IT was not without a degree of trepidation that Scottish Tory high-ups, including chairman Michael Forsyth, headed up the rock to Stirling Castle to attend one event on Margaret Thatcher's Scottish programme. They knew the schedule had leaked out, to the advantage of anti-poll tax demonstrators.

But to everyone's surprise, only about 30 demonstrators turned out at Stirling and things went off without any drama.

Later, Michael Forsyth mentioned this curious turn of events to Malcolm Rifkind, who had gone instead to address local Tories in Dunfermline. Rifkind was not amused: he had been confronted with 300 demonstrators.

It later turned out that the anti-poll tax campaigners had been convinced the Stirling do was a blind, and that Maggie would be in Dunfermline with Malcolm. The more the police on duty assured them the PM wasn't coming, the more they believed she was.

Was this a new tactic for the Summer of Discontent?

PRESIDENT DANIEL ORTEGA'S visit to Edinburgh City Chambers was not made, as some cynics suggested, just to thank the Labour administration for insisting that everyone at the Big Hoose drank Nicaraguan coffee. Indeed, representatives from other parties had access to the president as he worked his way round the crowded reception.

One of these was David Graham, representing the Scottish Social and Liberal Democrats and wearing his little diamond-shaped lapel badge. When the time came for him to be introduced, President Ortega peered at the badge while his interpreter murmured its significance into the presidential ear.

At that point, the SLD representative heard a woman behind him address the president in Spanish, the words *un poco* figuring largely. He turned to her in protest, pointing out that far from being *un poco* his party accounted for nine of Scotland's 72 MPs and furthermore . . . At which point the lady broke in to explain she'd only been saying she spoke very little Spanish.

By this time, of course, the mystified president had moved on. He was probably dying to get home again, to some political stability.

A VERY subtle tale was apparently circulating over the Westminster teacups, about Mrs T's legendary forceful manner. It's a supposedly mythical conversation between a back-bencher and a former Cabinet Minister.

BB: 'Did you know that the Prime Minister is partially deaf?'

Ex-CM (astonished): 'Good heavens! How on earth did anyone find out?'

WHEN the Scottish Tories launched a manifesto for the Euro-elections, much energy was expended upon assuring media sceptics that there was absolutely no division in the ranks over European policy. 'No split,' confirmed Malcolm Rifkind, at the appropriately named venue, the Hospitality Inn, 'just a healthy debate within the party.'

If any scribbler was divested of doubts by this performance, it was somewhat undermined when a party official explained that there had been an unfortunate misprint in the document. 'On Page 3,' he said 'for "fragmentation" you should read "unity"' . . .

A SLIGHT ambiguity in the layout of *Hansard* gave us this intriguing insight from Written Questions — Late Night Sittings (Costs):

Mr Allen: To ask the Lord President of the Council what estimate he has made of the costs of keeping the House open for sittings which go beyond 10 p.m.

Mr Wakeham: When a sitting of the House goes beyond 10 p.m. a wide diversity of costs are incurred. Spirits, 1.6 billion. Beer, 2.1 billion. Wine, 0.7 billion. Made wine, 0.1 billion. Cider and perry, 0.1 billion.

On closer scrutiny, it turned out that the table of figures belong to another answer on excise estimates. We thought we were on to something there.

IT may have come as some embarrassment to Sir Nicholas Fairbairn (but on the other hand, it might not) to learn of the part he played in raising money to unseat his Edinburgh West colleague, Lord James Douglas-Hamilton.

The Edinburgh West Lib Dems operated a second-hand stall in Edinburgh's Grassmarket to boost their election fighting fund. And there, among the bric-à-brac, was a painting signed by 'Nicholas Fairbairn, 1958'.

Probably for political reasons, it was not generally admired. After some debate, it was concluded to be a South of France landscape. It raised a modest £15. The big mystery was where the painting came from, as no one would admit to handing it in.

But then we discovered more of the picture's provenance.

It was handed in by Veronica Crerar, the Lib Dem councillor for Corstorphine South-East. We learn this because a couple of years before she had offered to sell it to her neighbour, Hamish Strang, then the local Tory chairman and therefore an ideologically sound prospect. He told us: 'Actually I declined it, but it did seem to be worth more than £15.'

Mrs Crerar told us that as the Lib Dems were setting up their stall, they were visited by the inevitable dealer, hunting unknown masterpieces. He declared the painting 'a good composition for an amateur'. But when asked to make an offer he, too, declined. However, it went at last — to an unknown home, strangely enough.

JIBES have been heard in the House of Commons over the parochial issues that occasionally surface during Scottish Question Time. There is a suspicion that some English MPs wait around for their own lofty amusement. They were not disappointed when Lord James Douglas-Hamilton, the Scottish Environment Minister, was asked about conservation projects being undertaken by the Forestry Commission.

There was a wide range of these on the way, he replied. Could he please give some examples? Indeed, the Minister had a little list in the best Gilbert and Sullivan tradition, and he began to read it out.

'Regenerating native pine roots,' he said. 'Constructing ponds . . . erecting batboxes . . . managing open rides for butterflies . . . creating clearings for lizards . . . planting broad-leaves for diversification . . . building bolts for otters . . .'

To judge by the hilarity on the Tory benches, it was one of the most successful replies of its kind.

COMPUTER users know all about 'a bug in the system', but this one is rather alarming. It cropped up at the Scottish Tory Central Office, where staff were equipped with new hardware.

Every so often, as the workers applied themselves to the task of improving the party standing in these northern badlands, the Apricot computer inserted a rogue line — in Cyrillic script. This was, of course, the alphabet of the KGB and countless other Russians.

Until the bug was sorted out, Scottish Tory *apparatchiks* had good reason to keep looking over their shoulders.

UNUSUAL gremlins appeared to be listening in when Malcolm Rifkind was being interviewed about a speech he had made to the Adam Smith Institute. The former Scottish Secretary was in the special BBC Scotland radio studio at Dover House, his London branch office. His inquisitor, political correspondent Iain MacWhirter, was talking to him down the line from Glasgow.

At a key point in their conversation, they were mysteriously interrupted by a commentary on the 4.30 race at Ripon — the service provided for bookmakers' shops. Falcon's Down was coming in at 12–1 ahead of Lanzarote (7–4 favourite) and Wine Cellar (11–2). Until the excitement was over, the interview with the Scottish Secretary had to go back again under starter's orders.

The point to be resolved was this: were Malcolm Rifkind's words being picked up in the nation's betting shops? He was talking about Capitalism propelling Britain ever onward, and the stakes being high. There could have been some confused punters hurriedly looking for these runners in the form book.

WHEN the National Union of Civil and Public Servants ran a competition among its members to design a new emblem for the Department of Social Security, the winning wit, from Liverpool, submitted this:

ALTHOUGH inquirers in the public interest discovered nothing remotely scandalous about George Bush during a previous US Presidential, an agency headline turned up reading: 'George Bush "Collapsed Naked in Savoy".' Aha. This revelation came from a new book, *The Winning of the White House*, by the editors of *Time* magazine.

However, Bush's collapse came at the Savoy Hotel, London, in 1960 while he was in the oil industry and he passed out when suffering from an ulcer. 'I was alone, naked, lying on the floor trying to reach a buzzer,' said the President. We knew it would be fairly boring.

THE *House Magazine*, that blameless journal which circulates among Members of Parliament and parliamentary staff, came up with an interesting tale concerning Tory MP Hugh Dykes (Harrow East).

Apparently, on a visit to an old folk's home in his constituency he singled out one resident for a special greeting. According to the report, he said: 'Here is a wonderful dear old white-haired lady. Let me say Hello to you . . . ' Upon which the lady is quoted as saying: 'B....r off, you old sod. I'm Labour.'

We are not sure if this rates as a public opinion poll. But, despite the magazine's usual coverage of weighty issues, this is the story which was being most often retold in the bars and dining-rooms.

WHEN Donald Dewar described the Edinburgh councillor Christine Richard as 'a stout Tory' he certainly started something. The shadow Scottish Secretary made his remark during a live television discussion: he was immediately pulled up for his apparent discourtesy and protested that of course he meant stout-spirited, not stout-fat.

But the appellation refused to go away and the lady received a letter addressed to 'Cllr Christine Richard, A Stout Tory, Edinburgh City Chambers'. That's the bad news. The good news is that it was only somebody wanting her to get the Stone of Scone restored to Scotland.

SOMETHING equally baffling took place north of Inverness. According to an advertisement in the *Ross-shire Journal*, the local Liberal Democrats hired the Labour Party's star turn to enliven their social gathering with a speech:

ROSS, CROMARTY & SKYE LIBERAL DEMOCRATS

ANNUAL BUFFET DANCE

with the

JOHN SMITH SOUND

NATIONAL HOTEL, DINGWALL

B U S I N E S S

HERE'S a cautionary tale from the world o' business. Probably fictitious, but never mind.

A Scottish electrical manufacturer quoted for a big North Sea job. The company didn't get the whole job but only part of it. Eventually, the boss of the main contractors called to see how the work was proceeding.

Lunchtime came and, of course, the visitor was taken out for a meal. The car stopped, out everyone got, but the visitor halted in his tracks and said: 'You're not taking me to a Wimpy, are you?'

'Well,' came the reply, 'we put the lunch out to tender and this was the lowest offer.'

HAVE you insulted a bank manager lately? Apparently, the trick is to go in hard, use Shakespeare, and not be afraid of excess hyperbole. Timing helps too.

The major banks were smarting under criticism from high places that they had been extracting rather too much in charges from small businesses and private clients. This was clearly in the mind of a Diary reader who found himself the victim of a cheque-is-in-the-post situation, as a result of which his current account slipped into overdraft . . . but only for 24 hours.

Bang, wallop — his bank immediately slapped on charges for all transactions, retrospective and otherwise, during the accounting period. For our correspondent it was a considerable sum.

He wrote to his bank manager. This rate of usury, he suggested, was so iniquitous that 'it would have Shylock slavering over his gaberdine'.

The bank manager wrote back. This literary allusion was so powerful, he said, that he would cancel the charges to demonstrate that 'the quality of mercy is not strained'.

So there you are. 'You shall have your desires with interest,' as the Bard said in *Henry IV* Part 1.

BY their acronyms ye shall know them — and you might be forgiven for thinking that marketing people are obsessed with the expense-account lunch. Not only do they have MEAL (Media Expenditure Analysis) but also CAVIAR (Cinema & Video Industry Audience Research).

HANDS up anyone who hasn't had to wait at home all day for workmen to arrive? See — nobody. Indeed James McKinnon, former President of the Institute of Chartered Accountants in Scotland, was talking about this very nuisance in London.

'I waited around all day for the gasman to come and fix a new meter, but he never turned up,' he declared. A further appointment proved no more successful: the gasman took one look at the McKinnons' German Shepherd dog and was never seen again.

What made Mr McKinnon's experience different from anyone else's is that he, too, was a sort of watchdog: Director General of Gas Supply, with the full power of statute to rap British Gas over the knuckles for any lapse in service to consumers since privatisation. He mentioned his experiences after presenting his annual report.

You'd expect British Gas to try harder for him, but he explained he deliberately put his account under another name so that he got the same service as everyone. His deputy, however, did not. So presumably *he* got five-star treatment?

Mr McKinnon shook his head: 'He waited around all day for the gasman to come and . . . ' Say no more.

KEEN and raring to go, some students turned up at an Edinburgh hotel for a three-day residential Manpower Services Commission course. Unfortunately, there was no sign of the lecturer, who was based in Sheffield. Contacted by phone, he said — oops, sorry — he'd got the dates wrong. He advised everyone to go back to their jobs for the rest of the day.

This was not universally possible, as some of them had travelled to Edinburgh from the Highlands and Islands.

Subject under study: Organisation & Management.

THE Diary's Business and Drama Correspondent was amused to find at the annual general meeting in Glasgow of Lilley, the construction group, that chairman Lewis Robertson was supplied in advance with a written script. This included such scorching lines as 'Thank you, Mr Miller' and 'If there is no other business, I now declare the AGM closed and would cordially invite you all to join us for lunch.'

There was some voting, of course, with 13 motions to be considered, and in each case the script ran as follows:

May I have a show of hands please?
Those in favour?
Any against?
I declare the motion carried (unanimously / by a majority) or (as poll procedure).

One thing was for sure: the script wasn't anticipating any trouble from the shareholders, and indeed none materialised. Perhaps the time is coming when the average board of a public limited company will have as many librettists as it has accountants.

IMPOLITE after-dinner joke, told by a West of Scotland type: Question: 'How do you end up with a small fortune?'

Answer: 'Start with a large one and employ an Edinburgh stockbroker.'

ECONOMICS concerns itself with the production and distribution of wealth: but that's still no excuse for helping yourself to the cutlery.

The Royal Bank of Scotland organised an economics conference in its offices in St Andrew Square, Edinburgh at which — no doubt — the latest theories on supply and demand, allocation of resources etc were being bandied about by the guests. Lunch, of course, was taken.

Afterwards one delegate, a local academic, arrived home to discover to his acute embarrassment that he had accidentally made off with a knife from the Royal Bank's dining-room.

He sent it back by post to a member of the bank's economics team, asking if it could possibly be slipped back quietly into the catering system, with no questions asked.

After the staff member had recovered from the shock of getting a knife through the post (there's some heavy symbolism in that kind of thing) the item of cutlery was restored to its place. There was no word of whether the bank was counting its forks.

LIVING as they do so close to the big atomic kettle at Dounreay, members of Wick Business & Traders' Association thought it would be interesting to hear why they should support the nuclear power programme in the face of opposition by anti-nuke activists.

So they were given a talk by a retired senior official of the Atomic Energy Authority, who spoke of a clean, efficient and safe plant which pumped £30 million a year into the local economy.

What about Chernobyl? He even had a light-hearted answer for that.

He said the accident at Chernobyl in the Ukraine, which caused radioactive fallout to rain down over a huge area of Europe, had been good news for some Lapland residents. 'If you happened to be a reindeer,' he said, 'people suddenly stopped shooting you.'

Er, quite. We gather that the traders' sense of humour held firm, and they passed a motion to fight threatened cuts at Dounreay.

FOR reasons best known to themselves, Edinburgh's city fathers and mothers requested a print-out of all Lothian firms involved in the defence industry. Hi-tech activities abounded — from 'ship roll stabilisation systems' to 'custom designed infra-red spectral photometers'. But between 'ferrous and non-ferrous electroplating' and 'hydraulic drive systems for marine and submarine use' came one of the longest-established defence jobs of all: 'Sporran manufacturing'.

IRISH jokes are supposed to be bad form: but what are we meant to think when they are being encouraged by the Irish themselves?

The Dublin magazine *Business & Finance* launched the following dubious competition. 'Firing of Weapons by Gardaí Covered by Precise Set of Rules,' (*Irish Times* headline).

'Scurrilous suggestions are being heard that the rules consist of (1) Form circle, and (2) Open fire. Do readers have any other ideas? Let us know.' Dearie me.

INTERESTED in a career in catering? The West of Scotland College in Ayrshire offered one which seemed to deal with the well-known meal involving two slices of bread:

HND FOOD TECHNOLOGY
(Sandwich course with electives)

A KIRK minister of our acquaintance, who likes to keep his sense of the ridiculous well honed, has the following letter pinned to the wall of his office:

'*To*: Jesus, Son of Joseph, Carpenter's Shop, Nazareth.

'*From*: Jordan Management Consultants, Jerusalem.

'It is our opinion that the 12 men you have picked to manage your new organisation lack the background, educational and vocational aptitude for the type of enterprise you are undertaking. They do not have the team concept.

'Simon Peter is emotionally unstable and given to fits of temper. Andrew has no qualities of leadership. The two brothers James and John place personal interest above company loyalty. Thomas demonstrates a questioning attitude that would tend to undermine morale.

'We feel it our duty to tell you that Matthew has been blacklisted by the Greater Jerusalem Better Business Bureau. James, the son of Alphaeus, and Thaddaeus have radical leanings, and both registered high on the manic-depressive scale.

'One of the candidates, however, shows great potential. He is a man of ability and resourcefulness, has a keen business mind and contacts in high places. He is highly motivated and ambitious. We recommend Judas Iscariot as your controller and right-hand man.

'We wish you every success in your new venture.'

FOR its new corporate identity, Edinburgh chartered surveyors Kenneth Ryden and Partners agreed to call itself, simply, Ryden. After consideration, it decided not to follow the fashionable practice of using an acronym.

A DAIRY company in Edinburgh decided to take some firm action against shoplifters.

A notice displayed prominently in the firm's shop read: 'Any youngsters found putting their fingers into the pots of yoghurt will have them cut off.
— The Management.'

FISHERMEN who work from the little harbours along the East Neuk of Fife are nothing if not survivors. Bad weather had kept their boats tied up for the best part of a month, giving them an enforced holiday. Fine — but if you're not earning anything, how can you go for a pint with your friends?

Some of them came up with an answer: geese. They went out shooting wild geese and sold them for beer money. It got to the stage where goose-weighing and goose-bartering became an everyday occurrence in the fishermen's pubs in Crail, Pittenweem and Anstruther.

At Pittenweem's West End Bar, the Diary learned: 'We've had fishermen coming in with carrier bags full of geese. You learn not to be surprised any more. When you go to the butcher's for some bacon, he'll almost certainly offer you goose instead.'

Meanwhile, out in the Forth estuary, the lobsters and crabs were having a bit of a holiday too.

FROM the wonderful lateral-thinking world of the life assurance companies:

Norwich Union offered those who joined its Funeral Expenses Plan a free gift — the most interesting of which was a bedside radio-alarm clock.

The Norwich also sent a circular to its customers with the following startling posthumous promise: 'If you die by natural causes within the first two years of the plan, we will pay you one-and-a-half times the premiums you have paid.'

ELECTRONICS engineers at Glasgow University might unwittingly popularise some new phrases with their invention of 'the world's fastest switch for fibre optic communication'. It operates at 10 *pico-seconds!* A pico-second is one millionth of a millionth of a second. And they hoped to make it still faster, perhaps to around 10 *femto-seconds*. A femtosecond is one thousandth of a picosecond.

All this could give rise to new phrases like 'Yes, madam, I'll be with you in a femtosecond' or 'Due to circumstances beyond our control, the train now arriving on Platform 14 is six pico-seconds late.' Or early, as the case may be.

THE hologram of Shakespeare's portrait — which the banks chose for their cheque cards, to the dismay of literary-minded Scots — caused great confusion.

A Royal Bank of Scotland branch heard from the elderly mother of one of its customers who was working abroad. She phoned to say the bank had sent him the wrong cheque card as the picture was of 'an old bald gentleman' who didn't resemble her son at all . . .

A READER'S anxiety quotient increased with the arrival of a sales pitch from the Woolwich Building Society about its new 'Accidental Death Plan' available only to 'selected customers'.

Our reader inquired: 'Why me? Do they know something I don't?'

SCIENTIFIC innovations are often achieved by boffins using the most unlikely equipment. At the Edinburgh Science Festival, an example of this was provided by Professor Brian Wherrett, of the Chair of Opto-Electronics at Heriot-Watt University, outlining research in the use of light rather than conventional electronics in computers.

One problem, he explained, lay in finding materials with a specific optical quality, called bistability. He sought help from colleagues with chemicals skills, who baffled him with long names and complex formulae. Tiring of this, he told them one day he would continue working with 'TSSB' and 'TSBB'. They gave him knowing nods and departed.

Professor Wherrett then disclosed to his Science Festival Audience that TSSB stood for Top Secret Small Bottle while TSBB was Top Secret Big Bottle. The first contained the Glenfiddich malt whisky and the second champagne. In time, he discovered that champagne — while optically good — tended to eat into the equipment. The malt whisky worked better although an Eastern European scientist, who copied the experiment without being told the nature of the liquid involved, actually complained about the smell.

However, Professor Wherrett recalled one advantage of his secret compounds. 'If you didn't like the calculations,' he said, 'you could always drink the computer.'

BUSINESS sign spotted in Cairo. Would you buy a used car from these people?

THERE'S a dire shortage of estate agent jokes, oddly enough. Trevor Kent, president of the National Association of these maligned types, appealed for quips on the profession so that he could collate them into a book in aid of charity.

But the response was poor. There's: (1) 'Why doesn't an estate agent look out of the window in the morning? — Because that would leave him nothing to do in the afternoon.' (22 of these submitted.)

Then there's: (2) 'My estate agent's called Rhino. He's thick-skinned, short-sighted and — boy — he knows how to charge.' (Also oversubscribed.)

Most of the jokes sent in have come from estate agents rather than the general public. Kent came to the odd conclusion that this proves estate agents aren't the least-liked professionals in the country after all.

THE Scottish CBI chairman Alistair Mair had mixed feelings, we suspect, when he welcomed council members to one particular meeting.

Apparently, there's a policy of calling these gatherings at various venues throughout Scotland, and on this occasion it had been decided to use the boardroom of St Johnstone FC at McDiarmid Park, Perth.

Mair told members of the council: 'Business is like sport: it's about successful competition. And who demonstrates this better in recent times than St Johnstone.'

Did his voice tremble at this point? It so happened that Mair was an ardent

Halifax, the UK's largest building society last week shut 234 of its 80 estate agency branches in London, but denied it was getting out of the estate agency business.

Aberdeen fan, and here he was at the very place where Saints, the Premier League newcomers, announced their spectacular arrival by walloping his beloved Dons by five goals to nil.

And to make matters worse, some of the boardroom trophies had been supplied by Mair's own company, Caithness Glass. Hah.

Business Women
PERTH branch of the Federation of Business and Professional Women will welcome Jackie Reeves as guest speaker, in the City Mills Hotel on Tuesday, at 7.30 p.m. The meeting is open to all interested women.

Jackie will give a demonstration of flower arranging.

READERS of the *Housing Association Weekly* are probably still puzzling over the little conundrum reproduced above. But even that one had nothing on the muddle Stirling District Council got into when its members attempted to unclog the machinery. We came across an item in the minutes which reported:

'Urgent Items — This item was brought forward by the Chair for consideration as a matter of urgency, on the grounds that action was required in respect of the increasing number of urgent items being submitted at meetings.

'Decision — To instruct the Chief Executive to ensure that only matters of genuine urgency are submitted to meetings as items of urgent business.' Try working that one out.

WHEN the Romanian people took over their country from the Ceausescus, one of the great perks was access to the Securitate files.

But something of a similar nature happened in Aberdeen, where a communications company specialising in the oil industry was bought out by a group of senior managers in a multi-million-pound deal.

The new managing director of the personnel division was able to call up all the personnel files for the previous ten years, and out of curiosity he had a look at his own.

To his great amusement, it said: 'Not suitable for management.'

WE were charmed to note a planning application that came before Dover District Council. It concerned a project at Redhouse Wall Poultry Farm, Sholden: 'Change of use from poultry shed to six holiday chalets.' Should bring the tourists flocking.

THE business magazine *Bits & Pieces*, circulating only in the United States and Canada, hoped to spread its wings elsewhere.

The Diary was thoroughly intrigued by the effusive description of the magazine's editor contained in the publicity leaflet:

'One of the secrets of *Bits & Pieces* is our editor, a pleasant chap with some grey in his hair and a twinkle in his eye.

'Perhaps we should also mention,' the leaflet goes on 'the world of experience under his belt.'

Golly.

GLASGOW UNIVERSITY was appealing to its graduates near and far to help it raise £50 million in five years. Glossy brochures, including covenant and loan forms, were being sent out, and one Scot was reaching for his chequebook when he read the small print on the last page. It said the brochure was designed and produced by a firm with a Manchester telephone number. The surge of generosity died before it reached his pen.

EYE-CATCHING adverts to revive the flagging property market were the order of the day. But how about this intriguing description of a new house found in Scottish *Homebuyer's Guide*: 'An unusual design from Wimpey Homes; note the widows above the front door.'

AN ENGLISH software company was advertising a post in *Current Vacancies for Graduates*. It would be useful to have a knowledge of one or more European languages, for example, 'German, French or Swiss . . . '

INTERESTING examples of foodspeak from *Food Processing* magazine. It highlighted a bakery and confectionery exhibition in Paris with the gripping title 'Europain 92'. On the same page, it warned us of some dangers that lurk in the wonderful world of nosh processing:

Water jacketed hoppers and product bores

ALL mortgage-payers groaning under the yoke of interest rates will love this idea from Japan. The Nippon Housing Loan company introduced the 100-year home loan, under which the purchasing couple pay interest only. There are special arrangements for their children and grandchildren to pay off the rest. Try it on a bank manager near you — NOW!

Another idea that could ease the cash flow came from the US. *Business* magazine reported that a supermarket chain in Florida had sold 1,250 one-pound bags of autumn leaves at about £8 a time. The buyers were idiots from the northerly states who had settled in the south and become nostalgic every 'fall' for the leaves they used to wade through on their way to school.

Now entrepreneurs weren't even waiting for the leaves to drop: they were snipping them off the trees and bleaching them to bring out the autumn colours.

AN OLD rule in journalism is that you shouldn't call *a woman* a lady, as you would be making certain assumptions. This is why we enjoyed the lame excuse by a motorist who had knocked down a pedestrian. He wrote in his insurance claim: 'I misjudged a lady crossing the street.'

The insurance business seems to be all laughs, judging by the collection of 'highway howlers' published in the rather sombre-sounding newsletter, *Legal & General Shareholder*. There have been so many cockeyed claims that the company is actually bringing them out in book form. Some samples:

'We had completed the turn and had just straightened the car when Miss X put her foot down and headed for the ladies' loo.'

'I turned into my drive and hit a tree which wasn't there before.'

'I knocked the man over. He admitted it was his fault as he had been knocked over before.'

'I was doing 28 mph. I am positive of this as I was looking at the speedo when I hit him.'

But for making a crisis out of a drama, we have: 'As the motorcycle hit my car head-on, I closed my eyes. I opened them to see a torso and legs hanging over the windscreen and arms dangling over the rear window. I felt violently sick. After a few seconds both ends started moving and I realised there were, in fact, two people on the roof. Fortunately, neither was seriously hurt.'

SOME crafty advertising slogans spotted in the US:

'Improve your drive with a different set of woods.' (Tree nursery.)

'Take home some hot rolls.' (Carpet showroom, New Mexico.)

'Why don't you go away?' (Travel agent's, Cambridge, Mass.)

HERE'S a name that clearly means business in the fast lane. Penguin's new edition of *Management and Motivation* was co-edited by Victor H. Vroom.

IS shark-fishing hard on the feet? We learned from *Scottish Wildlife* magazine that the EC shark quota for the Norwegians 'has been arrived at by looking at what they were able to catch in previous years, not on any scientific assessment of the current state of their socks.' Thank goodness for that.

CHAIRMAN JIMMY BURNETT offered some sage advice during a meeting of Edinburgh District Council's housing committee. Various tenders for an electrical contract were being considered, and it seemed that the winning bid by a huge margin — about £50,000 lower than anyone else's — had been submitted by ScottishPower.

But council officials thought that it would be a good idea to check. They learned that ScottishPower had discovered 'major arithmetical errors' in its tender, which would have to be withdrawn. This, observed Burnett, seemed as good a reason as any to check your electricity bills . . .

A TRADE forum was launched with the object of promoting links between Scotland and Finland.

So the Finnish trade commissioner in Scotland, Timo Auvinen, sent out a newsletter called *Finnfacts* which included a cartoon by Kari, described as Finland's favourite cartoonist. It showed a wild-eyed character waking up after a bad dream. The caption read: 'The nightmare of a united Europe . . . of British cooking, French whisky, German humour, Scandinavian television programmes, Spanish watches, Swiss bull-fighting, and the Italian army in charge of defence.'

The Finns are described as enthusiastic Europeans.

ONE thing about Rotary clubs is that they go out of their way to welcome to their lunch tables visiting members from other clubs around the world. When this happens, the president of the host club will have a list of the visitors' names and of their clubs, which he will read out before the soup comes round.

According to the Edinburgh *Rotary Bulletin*, this is where the problems can start. The accurate pronunciation of foreign names by local presidents is important, to avoid embarrassment.

The newsletter warned: 'The Japanese seaport of Fukuoka has a flourishing Rotary club. The last visitor from there was in 1976. By the law of averages, the next one will be along soon. So beware.'

ANIMALS

NOT everybody has trouble digesting SNP policy statements. Take Kathleen Jones's rabbit, for example.

Ms Jones wrote from Shropshire to MP Margaret Ewing's office, asking for the SNP's stance on defence, North Sea oil and gas, blood sports and electoral reform. This was to help in her studies for a degree in politics and psychology.

The material was duly sent, but Ms Jones was soon in touch again. 'Unfortunately,' she lamented, 'I left the material lying around at the close of the day and a substantial amount was eaten by my rabbit during a night raid.' Could the SNP, perhaps, replace the stuff? She promised to protect it from her voracious pet this time.

As compensation, she sent the SNP some home-made sweets which she made to raise funds for her local wildlife hospital. 'They were delicious,' said an SNP spokesman, licking his lips. But what really cheered everyone up was the idea of a rabbit eating its way through the blood-sports paper.

FROM the seabed off the fair western isle of Gigha, shellfish are brought to the tables of the discerning. But the diners in one Glasgow restaurant were rather taken aback to see the menu on the blackboard offering 'Ghia Scallops'.

The latest thing, no doubt, in designer fast-food.

A LETTER to the *West Cumberland Times & Star*, by a pigeon-fancier whose birds were too often being picked off by hawks, was signed 'G. Falcon'.

THE civilised world is divided into two groups: cat-lovers and those who think cat-lovers are bonkers. The Diary doesn't want to take sides here, merely to widen the debate by drawing attention to a book promoted under the headline 'How to talk to your cat'.

The publisher of *Your Talking Cat* took a full-page advertisement in *Competitors' Companion*, obviously expecting to find some kindred spirits among those who tear the labels from soup tins and wake up in the middle of the night to jot down slogans. The ad told us that there were 19 different ways a cat can say 'meow', and each has its special meaning. Cats also talk in body language.

The book includes evidence from a celebrated cat-assisted therapist about her hundreds of documented experiences creating 'conversations' between cats and people. Among the essential questions that are answered:

- How your cat sizes up your friends;
- Why your cat doesn't like to be stared at, yet sometimes stares at you;
- Why your cat may panic if you oversleep.

The book includes a *cat talk chart* translating the cat's language. 'Think of it,' enthuses the writer, 'no more being totally ignored by your independent cat.' Fine: but we foresee problems. What happens when your cat bans you from watching *Tom & Jerry*?

IT was a great relief that biological or chemical agents were not used in the Gulf War. But it may be interesting to learn that until recent years the Russians could supply respirators for horses and dogs.

A British War Office recognition manual on Soviet equipment — taken off the restricted list — showed what the well-protected pooch should look like.

IN white southern Africa, 'Keep Out' notices were a familiar feature of the landscape. With the coming independence of Namibia, however, one that greeted callers to the HQ of the South African Defence Force 201 Battalion would be consigned to the scrapheap. It read:

MILITARY AREA
NO TRESPASSERS.
SURVIVORS WILL
BE PROSECUTED.

But friendly warnings of this kind are unlikely to disappear from the hinterland of apartheid. A house in Johannesburg sprawled behind a notice reading: 'Savage Dog. Trespassers Will Be Eaten.'

AND here's another. But, in fact, the pooch turned out to be quite friendly. It simply had the unenviable job of guard dog in a crocodile camp at the Okavango Delta, Botswana.

DOG and cat rental is a thriving new business in Tokyo, reported *Marketing Week*. One agency rents out the little darlings at about £24 a day (with a £250 deposit) getting most of its hires from TV production companies. 'But young women are showing interest in Yorkshire terriers as costume accessories,' said the magazine, keeping a commendably straight face.

THE distinctive Belted Galloway bull, which was replaced as the tourism symbol for Dumfries & Galloway, despite local opposition, registered its disgust in the most comprehensive way.

One of the stylish two-tone beasts was taken to Edinburgh to make its mark (literally) on the playing fields of the Mary Erskine School, in poshest Ravelston, before various distinguished and influential guests.

It was a fund-raising idea by Margaret Wright, a farmer's wife in Stranraer, who had two daughters at the school.

The school playing fields were marked out in squares, the squares 'sold' to any takers, and the bull paraded around until the great moment when he lifted his tail. The owner of the desecrated square won the lottery.

The bull which performed this highly public service was the two-year-old Netherwood Norman, borrowed for the occasion from West Lothian farmer William Storrie, vice-president of the Belted Galloway Cattle Society.

There was also a plan to borrow a goose as well, to mark the turf for a booby prize. The barnacle goose is the new symbol which the Dumfries & Galloway Tourist Board introduced in place of the cherished 'Beltie'.

Some idea. Maybe, like Norman, they should have dropped it.

THERE are too many dogs in the Commons (official). This was, at least, the view of the services committee, whose members had a long meeting with the Serjeant-at-Arms to discuss the crisis.

It seems no fewer than 18 pooches, mutts and curs of various shapes and sizes were regular attenders at Westminister, and this is regarded as too many. One of the best-known media props was Bryan Gould's West Highland terrier Angus, who stays in the office with Mrs Gould (his secretary) when his master goes to the chamber. Then there's Austin Mitchell's unspecified terrier Yogi.

The committee resolved that enough was enough. No new dogs were to be allowed in. And the 18 who already brought their pets to Westminster were to be discouraged and asked to find alternative arrangements.

Meanwhile, the dogs that had established a pawhold in the corridors of power had to be registered with the Serjeant-at-Arms. Dog registration by the back door! Wasn't this one of the pet causes Mrs Thatcher fought against?

EDINBURGH Tory councillor Moira Knox's poodle, Pinto, had a sort of notoriety around the City Chambers, where it once dampened the carpet and earned an accolade in the Diary. But its fame spread even further.

The *Municipal Journal* reported that on his first hearts-and-minds visit to Scotland as Prime Minister, John

Major was reintroduced to Councillor Knox. She recalled their previous meeting in Edinburgh, when he was Chancellor.

'Ah yes,' he said, 'I remember. There was a poodle there and it peed on the chair.' Not the *ideal* way of being noticed by the First Lord of the Treasury, but it certainly worked.

This may have been a Freudian slip. But when Mrs Knox was being ribbed by certain Labour councillors over her appointment to Lothian Health Board, she responded: 'I am not a political poodle.'

THIS tale starts with a small puddle in the Members' Lobby at Westminster — a puddle which, it must be said, did not escape the eagle eye of certain sections of the London *meeja*. Putting two and two together, they laid the blame at the feet — all four feet — of MP David Blunkett's guide-dog, Offa. And this heinous accusation duly appeared in two London-based newspapers.

When David Blunkett learned of this he was far from amused. Offa, he protested, was a paragon of the canine race and was (quite literally) fully House-trained. Not only that, but it had since come to light that the puddle was the result of a leaking — confirming the popular view that the fabric of the Palace of Westminster is fraying badly.

We hear that Blunkett was on the phone to the two newspapers concerned. Speaking on behalf of his dog, he requested a printed apology. To the best of our knowledge, no solemn retraction appeared.

Will Offa be the first dog to take a case before the Press Complaints Commission?

HERE'S a remarkable offer in the livestock columns of the *Inverness Courier*:

> 2 beautiful Highland Bollocks, 1 blond, 1 red, ideal attraction around Hotels and Parks, delivery can be arranged. Offers over £325 each. To view Tel . . .

HERE is useful information about how the mind of the average computer works. The medical magazine *Lancet* records the case of a young lady who wanted above all a career working with animals. But she lacked the qualifications for veterinary medicine.

She decided to buy advice from a 'careers computer'. She loved animals, she told it. She had no aversion to the sight of blood. The computer clicked, bleeped, and thought for a moment. 'Try butcher', it offered.

WE heard of a couple in Midlothian who discovered a stray polecat ferret — a tame animal which had obviously wandered off from a good home in search of pastures new.

They decided to advertise it under 'Found' in their local newsagent's window. But to their amusement, the notice was changed to read 'poll tax ferret'.

QUACKING good fun is enjoyed at the annual Stockbridge Duck Race in Edinburgh. The plan is to send a flotilla of plastic ducks — of the kind normally encountered in the bath — down the fast-flowing Water of Leith, and discover which one finishes first.

Once, however, the fleet of plastic toy ducks was joined by a live female mallard. She was floating along happily, well up with the leaders, when she seemed to realise the horrible significance of it all: one of the top prizes in this charity event was an item of oven-ready poultry. In fact, an oven-ready duck.

Suddenly she took off, every feather intact.

WE have moles everywhere, even in the small Lancashire town of Garstang. One of our observers had stopped there for a quiet coffee when he heard the squeal of brakes. A motorist had come round the corner to find a lethargic dog right in his path: and despite his quick reaction, the pooch suffered an almighty clout which seemed to remove it from any further interest in the proceedings.

The distraught motorist leapt from his car to attend to the dog (giving it the kiss of life, perhaps?) and as he knelt there the inevitable happened.

There was another squeal of brakes, and another thump, as a second car clobbered the first. It lurched forward, dealing the first driver a resounding blow to the head.

He too was knocked out — coming round after a few moments with the help of the dog which had by this time recovered and was applying first-aid by licking his assailant juicily on the face.

The unfortunate driver had to go to the local hospital for a check-up: and, we assume, a bath.

FROM the *Falkirk Herald*:

PURE Border Collie pups, 11 weeks, both parents can be seen, black/shite, £25. — Tel. Banknock 840273.

EVERY possible thing the hill farmer could need at lambing time was advertised in the *West Highland Free Press* by a helpful local pharmacy. The last item is probably aimed at the really sensible hill farmer:

LAMBING TIME

5 kilo EWE MILK REPLACER..........	£8.25
LAMB TEATS...........................	from 52p
MARKER SPRAYS.........................	£2.62
FOSTER LAMB AEROSOL............	£4.59
TEREBEME BALSAM.....................	£3.93

• *INSTANT COLOUR PASSPORT PICTURES* •

SOLEMN news from Edinburgh's Pilrig Park, where elderly people living in sheltered housing are sometimes troubled by playful dogs being exercised off the leash. They leap around a bit in a way that can be alarming to old folk. Dog owners, asked to keep their pets under control, have been known to say to the pensioners: 'It's you that should be on a leash.' This is not nice.

So the residents were pressing for a regulation obliging all owners to keep their dogs on a lead in the park. The matter was batted about between Lothian Regional and Edinburgh District councils, with a memo from one councillor to another using the memorable phrase: 'Can steps be taken to prevent pensioner-pouncing by poodles in Pilrig Park?'

We heard that the alliterative issue was receiving sombre attention.

EVEN German shepherd dogs are sensitive to public opinion. A sign on a garden gate in Crieff read:

'Hello, my name is Glenn. I would love to be petted, but due to the recent publicity regarding big dogs biting, please do not put your hand through the gates to play with me. I would prefer it if you just said Hello. Thank you.'

Coming soon: A Rottweiler hires Saatchi & Saatchi.

THE *Daily Record's* campaign against 'killer dogs' must have been working. It ran an editorial saying: 'No one should be able to keep a dog which is a nuisance to others, far less a deadly danger.' Turning to the advertising pages, we found no fewer than six people who had taken the hint and were offering to sell Rottweiler puppies.

IT'S a sad predicament, you might think, when cage birds manage to occupy the moral high ground. This headline is from the *Daily Telegraph*:

NOT everyone agrees with forestry policy in Scotland, and it looks as if objections are being registered by what the Gaels call the great cock of the wood. This, of course, is the capercaillie (*Tetrao urogallus*).

According to the Forestry Commission's curiously-named newsletter *The Slasher*, several forestry workers have been attacked by these enormous turkey-like creatures, game birds in more ways than one.

The attacks were reported from Perthshire. One victim, a civil engineering foreman, was trying to photograph a courting capercaillie, and the bird naturally took umbrage. It charged the offending photographer and knocked him flying.

Two other foresters were attempting to carry out an inspection of mature trees when the resident capercaillie, obviously realising that they had unwelcome plans for his territory, shooed them firmly away.

'I wasn't able to get out of the way as quickly as the bird wanted,' said one forester ruefully.

WE recall a time when the bird with the funny name was served as the main course at a glittering dinner in the

Canaries to ban bullfighting

Highland resort of Aviemore.

After the dinner, the capercaillie was followed by a ceilidh, and against the background din of fiddles and accordions, a photographer of our acquaintance was asked: 'Did you enjoy the capercaillie?'

'Yes,' he shouted back, 'but it's a bit loud.'

FROM the *East Lothian Courier*, we have *le mot juste*. The newspaper reported that ever-opportunist rabbits had been feeding on the floral tributes left by relatives at the new Innerwick cemetery. The community council chairman, Reggie Gibson, described this as 'a grave concern to the whole community'.

CURIOUS sign in the Braid Hills, Edinburgh, aimed at amorous equitation: 'All horses and ponies must stay on bridal path.'

THE hunt has obviously been successful. A multilingual reader of our hatched, matched and dispatched column pointed out that a Miss Tod (Scots for 'fox') had become engaged to a Signor Volpe (Italian for that very same animal).

THE retail food trade, at least, isn't hiding its head in the sand over the latest piece of bizarre gourmandism to threaten our dinner tables. Following an Oxfordshire couple's plan to establish a breeding herd of ostriches at their 60-acre farm, *The Grocer* magazine pointed out that this large flightless fowl is commonly cooked and served up in South Africa.

Useful facts: A single thigh will feed a football team with lean meat, claimed to be very low in cholesterol. A carcase will weigh 300 pounds and supply firm red meat, not white, which can be cooked to almost any recipe. A single egg will provide an omelette big enough for ten.

Then there are the peripherals: 'The feathers are highly prized for making dusters, while what remains often ends up as some of the tackiest souvenirs imaginable. The necks, for instance, can be dried, hardened and used as spaghetti jars. The legs have been topped out as free-standing ashtrays, while the toenails are made into jewellery. Ugh,' concluded the magazine.

It's not surprising, said the *The Grocer*, that the birds have a bone-breaking kick and an impressive turn of speed.

WE heard of an interesting change-of-use case for premises in Fairmilehead, Edinburgh. This used to be a butcher's shop, in which the butcher's name was tastefully displayed above the window between illustrations of a fat and contented pig and a beefy and languorous bullock. Well, the butcher has gone — but the pig and the bullock remain. Between them, however, is a new legend: 'Veterinary Surgery'.

THE *British Medical Journal* revealed that the farming community doesn't like journalists referring to BSE as 'mad cow disease'. Farmers would much prefer the popular name changed to 'anxious cow disease'.

A LECTURE bound to interest Scots feminists was held at Edinburgh University. Dr Liz Rogers spoke on 'Lowland gorillas: How different are they?'

SOMETIMES, life's a bitch. But this sign in the shop window shows that a chemist in Chester wants to have no part in it:

THE *Shetland Times* reported that a significant number of rabbits without tails had been sighted — or shot — in the Ness area. This news emerged as Shetland Islands Council was about to consider raising the bounty in its rabbit-control scheme from 25p to 35p for each bunny dispatched. In traditional fashion, the hunters are paid on each rabbit tail they hand over.

One shooter said he had already been stymied by copping five tailless rabbits — '£1.25 down the drain, you might say.' Is this a defensive form of evolution?

WAS it the ultimate protest against primary school testing? Who knows; but when Scottish Office minister Michael Forsyth visited Stewart's-Melville College in Edinburgh as part of his hearts-and-minds campaign, the pet guinea pig in the classroom next door rolled over and died.

The deputy principal had to be called away from the high-powered conclave to administer the last rites. A ministerial visit was a ministerial visit, but a deceased guinea pig was a major crisis, and some of the pupils were quite upset.

We hear that the parents who had been looking after the school rodent over the weekend reported that it had been looking rather sleepy. The cause of death wasn't announced, but incipient boredom can't be ruled out.

NEAR Fenwick, in Ayrshire, is a halt sign designed to be understood by horses:

WE note that the 1991 Vets' Congress in Torquay included a session about the pleasures of owning a pet —

'Healthy Animals, Good Companions' — with a talk being given by Ivan H. Burger.

IT was Sweep, the drug-sniffing collie, who stole the show during a ministerial visit to Cornton Vale women's prison, near Stirling.

Sweep was one of a quartet of pooches — collies and labradors — which were supposed to demonstrate their skills for their ultimate boss, Lord James Douglas-Hamilton, the Scottish home affairs minister, and a posse of *meejavolk*.

The idea was that a package of cannabis would be concealed in the prison chapel: but first of all Sweep made a quick circuit to show that the place was clean.

Instead, the canine detective spent rather a suspicious amount of time sniffing around the trouserleg of Our Man (whom we will call John Smith to protect anonymity) before going on to make an equally thorough investigation of the Lord Jamesian trousers.

They could be heard protesting loudly that they were both dog-owners and that no doubt this must have something to do with it. There were no arrests.

GREAT Suburban Hazards of Our Time: A rather alarming phone call reached an Edinburgh man at work. It was from his wife, at home in Corstorphine. The dog was having a funny turn. Its eyes were glazed, its legs were rubbery and it kept walking into things.

Back home dashed Our Man to handle the domestic crisis. But the first thing he did was rush upstairs and look under the bed — where he'd hidden a large box of chocolate liqueurs.

He was right. The drunken mutt had found them and scoffed the lot.

DIARY
Anthony Troon